If anyone tells you to respect a game, let this be your reply: "Two things are important in every game – a player and the rules of the game. A game is meant to be played. Thus, a game only needs a player. A game doesn't require respect, because it only results in two things in the end: a loser and a winner. A game doesn't produce respect."

A KING IS JUST AS IMPORTANT AS THE PEOPLE HE RULES.

THE

KING

OF

ALL

LIARS

Teni Abegunde

CATAPHRASE MIAB
www.cataphrase.com

ALSO BY TENI A.

The First Sit-Down Comedy

You will laugh. Guaranteed!

PRINTED IN THE UNITED STATES OF AMERICA

Published by Cataphrase MIAB, Washington, DC
www.cataphrase.com

9763—09 13 01 16 CA:097-342; 181875
Serial# 0773403-9 Log—1358L229/772
IMF courtesy—0717V2

0A1—0726/A113-2018

Paperback Edition,
ISBN:978-0-9916306-4-6
Ebook:978-0-9916306-9-1
The king of all liars / Teni Abegunde
The first sit-down comedy book / Washington DC
PNT Edition / VII-0067—033

AKNOWLEDGEMENTS

To those who served, and those who are still serving in the United States military, thank you. May God bless you and your families.

This year has been a wonderful year for me. I published two books including this one. My appreciation goes to all those who contributed to the success of these books.

Special thanks to the Washington Capitals for bringing the Stanley Cup to the place I call home. I know one day—*at least* before the world ends—the Washington Wizards and the Redskin will also make us proud.

*"When you open a book, you open
the mind of the author."*
—Teni A.

*"The road to becoming a successful man is
hard, I must confess. Yet I can guarantee
you one thing: if you teach your son
courage and hard work, he'll
figure out the rest."*
—Teni A.

*"If you meet a person who thinks everybody has
a problem except him or her, please stay
away from that person. Such a human
has an incurable problem."*
—Teni A.

Some people say that life is a mystery. Some people say that life is hard. Many people say otherwise. As time goes by, life becomes a complex question that no one can answer. Where did life come from? What is the purpose of life? And how will life end? Just like you, I don't know the answers to these questions. But I know one thing: life is here, and among the living, I must survive.

I would like to thank you. Thank you very much for taking a moment out of your precious life to read the first sit-down comedy book.

If you are reading the hard copy version of this book, please pay no mind to the squirrel on the back cover. The title of this book was inspired by the fact that the funniest joke ever told is a lie. And, just like with politicians, lying happens to be one of the things I'm very good at.

Before I get started, let me tell you one or two things about myself. Of the three children my mother bore, I'm the only one who is left-handed. I'm not sure if this preference to the left hand was due to my dad not being Mr. Right, or due to nature deciding my fate without my consent.

I love fast cars and fast food. Though I can't afford a Bugatti right now, I can afford a buffet meal. Yet, as much as I love the fast life, I'm always careful, because I know that if a fast car doesn't kill you, fast food will.

I would love to be a vegetarian, just not in this lifetime. I mean, I'm simply not cool enough to enter Golden Corral, pay $13.99, and walk right past orange chicken, barbeque pork, steak and broccoli, buffalo wings, bacon, fried shrimp, and pepperoni pizza and straight to the salad bar. What am I, crazy? Even if I were out of my senses and ate a salad first, I'd still add grilled chicken or sliced eggs to it.

Nothing infuriates me more than when someone I trust lies to me, especially if they are close to me.

During my unrelenting search for people I can trust, I discovered a truth I had never thought of: there's a difference between someone lying to you and *you* failing to ask the right question. I was on trial one morning, just a day after my sixteenth birthday, when my lawyer said something to the judge that I didn't understand. Instead of asking my lawyer directly as to what he had meant, I ended up embarrassing myself in the courtroom. My lawyer had told the judge that I was "insane" when I had committed the crime. I interrupted the proceedings with an objection. Puzzled, the judge looked at me and said, "You are objecting your own defense, Mr. Teni?"

"Yes, Your Honor. There's something I need

to clarify before my lawyer proceeds. Your Honor, I wasn't in Sane when this incident happened. I was in America. I don't know where Sane is. I've never been to that country before. Your Honor, I was at a cafeteria in El Paso, Texas, when I got arrested—not Sane."

Later in this book, I will discuss the topic of dating. Nevertheless, let me make a point before I continue. Ladies, I know that I haven't dated all of you. However, I've dated enough times to notice that most women don't know how to ask the right questions.

Ladies, not every man that you see driving a Mercedes-Benz is rich. If you meet a guy who drives a nice Benz, you need to ask him if he has cold hard cash, or if he just has good credit; because, you know, in these days, they'll give you anything if your credit is good.

Some ladies have ended relationships because they thought the guy they were dating had lied to them. He didn't, though – you were the one who failed to ask him the right questions when you first met him.

You had asked him where he worked, and he said he "worked at the bank." But did you ask him what he did at the bank? Was he a security guard, a teller, a robber, a janitor, or the manager?

You asked him what he drove, and he said "a Mercedes-Benz." Did you ask him what year his Benz was made? Was it a new model, or one that came out when Abraham Lincoln was President?

You asked him what kind of wristwatch he wears, and he said "Gucci". Did you ask if the Gucci was made in China, Mexico, or Paris?

Look, I know some questions are difficult to ask. So is accepting the truth. Learning the truth is hard, yet it's important to ask the right questions.

Also, it does not matter to me if people are good, nice, or bad. Rather, I like and prefer reasonable people. Reasonable people use logic and reason in judging every situation, whereas others only behave as they please.

Have you mistakenly hit another car's

bumper in a parking lot while reversing, and the driver in the other car wanted you to call the ambulance because their neck and back suddenly hurt, and they needed to see a doctor right away?

Along with insurance diggers, there are other things I hate: snowstorms, advertisements during playoff games, my former job, climbing a stairway, slow internet, traffic jams, doctor's appointments, etc.

However, above everything I despise in life, I hate poverty, even more so than death. Let me illustrate how much I hate poverty. Imagine this scenario: I'm relaxing on my front porch, with all my life savings and a loaded .357 in my hand. Suddenly, I see two enemies running towards me – one is after my life with shotgun in hand, and the other is after my life savings with just his bare hands. I would shoot the latter first before I shoot the one with the shotgun – that's how much I hate poverty.

Severe poverty can make a person of sound mind behave like a lunatic. Folks, have you ever seen a person standing in the middle of a busy three-lane highway, with cardboard in hand and begging for money? That's what poverty can turn a perfectly normal person into. It doesn't matter how smart a person is; poverty can make them behave like a moron. No one should be so broke to the point where they go to a dollar store and ask the cashier for a discount. The cashier would surely look at them and think, "Really? Sir, we've already reduced the price to a dollar. How much lower should we go?"

When I was young, my life was so screwed up because no one taught me the basic things in life. No one taught me how to swim, how to greet people, or how to ride a bike. Most of what I know today, I had learned through experience.

I can remember when I got my first job. Man, I was happy. During my interview, my then supervisor-to-be had told me that the job paid eight dollars per hour. So, I calculated how much I would earn if I worked eighty hours in two weeks. My calculation came up to six hundred and forty dollars.

On the day I received my first paycheck, I tore the envelope open like a starving raccoon. To my surprise, the figure I saw on the check wasn't what I had expected. My check was around two hundred dollars short of my calculation. I went straight to my supervisor's office, thinking someone was trying to cheat me. When I handed the check to her, she looked at it and said, "I don't see anything wrong with your payment."

"Ma'am, I worked eighty hours these last two weeks. My check is supposed to be six hundred and forty dollars," I replied.

She looked at the check again before looking at me. Then, she asked me a question I would never forget for the rest of my life.

"Mr. Teni, have you heard about taxes?"

"Yeah."

"Well, that's why your check is short."

"Which *taxes*? The ones Jesus and Peter paid in the Bible, or the ones we pay when we buy groceries at Giant?"

My complete ignorance about state and federal

taxes befuddled my supervisor for a moment. Then she asked, "Is this your first job?"

"Yeah," I replied.

"No wonder."

That was how the state and the federal government first introduced themselves to me.

You've got to love the United States. America is the only country in the world where homeless people wear Gucci belts. But it doesn't matter how much you love America; there will always be some small hatred for the state and the feds that crops up in you when you see the tax section of your paycheck. This is especially so after you've worked overtime, and they've charged you more on taxes, as if the money they borrowed from China was spent on your family alone.

The second time the feds introduced themselves to me, they found out just how much I hate abbreviations the hard way.

I had been a witness to a cop shooting a bank robber, so the feds came to my house the following day to ask me questions. First, I was mad because they knocked on my door at nine o'clock in the morning. Everybody in my neighborhood knows I don't wake up until 10 a.m. — that's when the mall opens. I woke up thinking my grandmother had found out about the girl I had impregnated. I was praying to Jesus as I approached the front door. When I got closer to the door, I whispered gently,

"Who is it?"

The person behind the door replied, "It's the FBI. Open the door."

"Who is the FBI?" I asked.

I believed that question upset him. He retorted, "You don't know what FBI stands for?"

"Yeah, I do. It stands for Fucking Bitch Idiots," I replied.

Have you ever looked at the tax section of your pay slip and seen an abbreviation you don't recognize taking money out of your check? Like, who the hell is OASDI?

If you ask me where the craziest place in America is, I would say Harlem. For those who are not familiar with Harlem, it is a large neighborhood in New York City. It's the place where Jesus turned water to wine. I'm just kidding. But seriously, strange things happen in Harlem.

The first time I visited Harlem, I had traveled from Maryland on a train to Manhattan and arrived around 8 p.m. From there, I took the subway to Harlem. Don't ask me why I went to Harlem, because I don't know. I was in New York for the first time, and I decided to visit a historical place.

When the subway arrived in Harlem, the operator made a paradoxical announcement that went something like: "Welcome to Harlem, the land of the free and the home of the brave. If you are sitting, sit tight. And if you are standing, make sure to hold the pole with one hand, and hold your bags and cellphones with the other." Now, if you were sitting inside a train car, and the operator gave such a specific announcement, you would likely think that something wasn't right.

Our first stop in Harlem was 116th Street

Station. Boy, that station was rough. I looked outside the window, and saw both humans and rats sitting on benches, waiting for the train. When the train finally came to a complete stop and the door opened, two men and a rat ran inside the car I was in. The roaches didn't bother to get on the train – they were too drunk. I mean, *w-a-a-ay* too drunk. You know roaches are drunk when they start flying, instead of running.

The two men who got on the train must have been drinking heavily too, because they did things that made me wonder if I was in a Looney Tunes cartoon, or if I was on my way there. A minute or so after the train took off, one dude placed a phone call with a banana. What baffled me wasn't the banana phone call, but what the hell the dude was saying. At first, he was having a conversation with his mother – which I guess, to him, was boring. So, he hung up on his mama and called one of his buddies with the banana instead.

"Hey, man. Our helicopter just crash-landed in Baghdad. But I'm good, bro. Hey, I'm about to defuse an IED. Did you know that the last one I had tried to defuse went off and killed me? So, man…I need you to pray for me this time." The moment he mentioned the IED, the old lady who was sitting beside him stood up and found a seat elsewhere. All of us around him were nervous, because he also had a backpack and we didn't know what it contained.

As if that wasn't enough, the other dude opened his guitar case, took out a fishing rod, and started fishing on the train. While he was struggling with the gear as though he were at the bay, he said something that made everyone sitting next to him stand up and leave. He turned to his friend with the banana and said, "Joe, I got something!" Then, he looked under his seat and exclaimed, "IT'S A SHARK!"

Sharks are scary no matter what context they are in. But the scariest thing, perhaps, is when your boss tells you to stop whatever you are doing and report to his office right away.

I was on duty one morning when my manager

came to me and told me to see him in his office before I took my first break. As soon as he left, I got on Indeed.com, and started filling out job applications. Incidentally, UPS had called me a week before, and I had told them that I already had a job. I called them back, and asked if they were still hiring.

Five minutes before my break, my heart beat fast, and my blood pressure rose. Finally, I got to my manager's office. For some reason, when you enter your manager's office, they always seem to be on the computer, and then look at you swiftly and ask you to sit down. That's exactly what happened with me. So, I took a seat. After several miserable seconds that felt like forever, he turned to me and asked, "What time did you clock out yesterday?"

"Three."

"Great. I just want to make sure you get paid for the hours you worked."

"Is that why you called me into your office?"

"Yeah, that's it. Why?"

"Man…"

14

By that time, my face had paled.

"Mr. Teni, what's wrong?" he asked.

"John, I scheduled an interview with UPS."

"Why?"

"I thought I was getting fired!"

Humans are the most intelligent living creatures on earth. I know some people would argue with this statement, but I'll wait until I see a dolphin or a chimpanzee attempt to create an iPad before I believe them. Yet, as intelligent as we are, we often behave unreasonably.

Has someone ever asked you a stupid question? By this, I mean a very stupid question – a question so stupid, you look at the person and ask if they really meant to ask you the question.

Every Friday, when I receive my paycheck, I go to the bank to cash it. One Friday, as I was standing in line inside a Bank of America branch and waiting to cash my check, a man came out of nowhere and asked if I was in line.

Folks, I don't know about you, but I hate stupidity. First, I gave him that three-second look, the one you get from a judge after he or she asks, "How do you plead?" and you reply, "Guilty with explanation."

Then, I turned away and pretended that I didn't hear him. Meanwhile, the line was moving. So, I moved with it. This dude had the nerve to ask me if I was in line a second time. I looked him straight in the eye and replied, "No, I'm not in line. I'm on the roof."

I've seen a lady walk up to a police patrol car—I'm talking about a clearly marked police car with LAPD signs written all over it—and asked the officer sitting inside if he was a cop. I didn't hear the officer's reply, but if I was him, my reply would have been: "No, I'm not a cop. I'm a stripper. I just put on this uniform and bulletproof vest because it's tight. What about you? Are you a human?"

In America, most of us like to ask dumb questions. I guess we are used to it. And the funniest part is that we don't even realize how dumb some of these questions are. For instance, imagine you are holding a huge python, and an

American sees you. They're likely to say something along the lines of: "Oh my God! Is that a snake?" Personally, I would reply, "No, ma'am, it's not a snake. It's a dinosaur."

Traffic court cases can often be hilarious. Folks, if you are guilty of something, you are guilty of it—you have no excuse. How in the world does a person plead guilty with explanation? That is like catching your cheating spouse red-handed, and they say, "Baby, I can explain." Explain what?!

Also, have you ever sat in traffic court, and while waiting for your name to be called, the judge explains to a Hispanic man – through his interpreter – that the police officer who had pulled him over is not present in court and that his case is therefore dismissed, yet the defendant still wishes to plead guilty? Huh?

Hispanic people are hilarious, especially Mexicans. One day, while at 7-Eleven, a Mexican man bought a scratch-off ticket and asked me to help him check if he had won any money. I was like, "Dude, if you don't understand how

17

this shit works, why the heck are you buying it?"

That reminds me of the day I won a hundred million dollars on a lottery ticket. The only problem I had was that I couldn't cash the ticket because I was dreaming.

This one here is called *Folks in America*. If you are not from America, don't worry, you can still relate to it.

I'll start with black folks. Black folks are cool; they just don't show it often. I won't use my mum as an example. But let me just say that I can't tell if my mum is white or black. She behaves like both, depending on the type of situation she's in. For instance, when she's at the bank trying to secure a loan, she can negotiate like a white person. But, God forbid you happen to be a cashier at the Popeyes where she had just ordered food, and you messed up her drive-thru order, so much so that she had to walk inside the restaurant to fix the problem herself. You can understand why certain American dishes are specifically referred to as "soul food."

Like I was saying, black folks are cool. But you will only discover how cool black folks are from the activities they'd deliberately abstained from, such as ice hockey, alpine climbing, ice fishing and unless a regular black person is high on something, trying to commit suicide; and if perhaps he or she is in the military, sky and ocean diving are also other activities you won't necessarily see the majority of black people participating in. And it's not as though black folks hate these activities and that's why they don't often participate. Black folks just seem to naturally appreciate life more than any other race on earth. That's why you will never see two black folks playing Russian roulette. Never.

And if you've witnessed a black person attempting Russian roulette, I guarantee you there's no bullet in that revolver.

White folks are cool too; and they like to show it. White folks are so cool they can sleep in a cooler and they won't freeze. For instance, the temperature outside could be minus fifty-degrees Fahrenheit, and white folks will still have the AC on inside their office. What will surprise you most is their reaction to seeing black folks at their job dressed like astronauts. For example, "John, what is wrong with Nicole? She had on a sweater, a jacket, a fur and a hoody at the meeting yesterday."

"Yeah, you're right. But do you know why?"

"No..."

"BECAUSE SHE'S FREEZING..."

One more thing before I round up on folks in America. White folks: it's cool to be cool, but it's not cool to be too cool. Let me get close and personal. White people, if you arrive at a crosswalk red light signal at 2 o'clock in the morning and you turn your head to the north and you don't see a car coming, and you turn your head to the south and don't see a car coming, and you look to the east and the west and you don't see a car coming but the crosswalk pedestrian signal light is still red, white folks... it's safe to cross the road.

I don't know why every movie that comes out

these days must have a gorilla in it. Have you noticed that too?

Back in the day, before zoos were built, watching monkeys used to be free. We didn't go to them; they came to us, and we gave them bananas and grapes. As humans became more civilized, we locked them up in zoos and occasionally go to watch them. Now, things have completely changed. If you want to see gorillas, you need to go to the movie theater. It seems as though apes are doing better than humans – they keep moving up! At this rate, we'll start to see them soon in our dreams.

At the beginning of the year, I told myself that if another gorilla movie comes out, I will stop watching movies. Three months later, *Rampage* came out. I wasn't interested in seeing the movie; but after I saw the trailer, I decided to give it a try.

At noon, I went to Regal Cinema, and asked the teller how much a ticket for a standard showing was.

"Thirteen dollars and some change," she

said, while looking at the computer screen.

"To watch a fake gorilla!"

"Er...it's a new movie."

"How much will it cost to see it in 3D?"

"Give me a second… Only seventeen dollars and fifty-nine cents."

"Oh, hell no! I'll wait for the bootleg to come out. Or I'll just go to a safari!"

"Your plane ticket to Africa will cost much more than our movie ticket."

"Then I'll go to the national zoo!" I replied.

But I remembered that my girl had called me earlier that day and insisted we watch it that night. So, I had no choice but to buy two tickets for both of us.

We went to the theater later that night, and part two of the arbitrary price tried to present itself. *You know what I'm talking about*! THE FOOD! The price of popcorn, chips, and soda for one person was around $25.99. Never mind the price of a burger and fries – it was approximately the same amount the feds deducted from my paycheck every two weeks.

I told my girl to go wait for me in the theater. "I'll join you shortly," I added. She headed to the cinema, while I went outside.

Ten minutes later, I entered the theater with bags full of food, and spread these on the tray table before her like God did for David in Psalm 23.

Once we were seated, she asked for her popcorn. I lied, and told her they'd run out of popcorn for the next hour. The movie came on, so the theater got a little bit darker. She couldn't see the labels on the bags in front of her. She nevertheless stuck her hand in the first bag, and started eating.

"Baby, these chicken tenders are good. They taste like Popeyes."

I didn't say a word. When she finished the tenders, she moved her hand over to the next bag, and took out a sandwich.

"Baby, this sandwich tastes like McChicken."

The fat, nosey dude sitting next to us replied before I could.

"Oh, yeah! I smell cheeseburgers, too. Is

there a Burger King in this movie theater?"

I said, "Nope. But if you walk three blocks down the street, they got a Popeyes, Burger King and McDonald's lined side by side on the boulevard. All for $6.99."

My girl asked, "You went to Popeyes?"

"Yes, I did."

She didn't know what to say. A few seconds later, she said, "Alright, baby, just get me something to drink."

Before she finished her sentence, I had already pulled out a six-pack of Old Milwaukee from my jacket, and placed it on the tray table. She said, "You went to the liquor store, too?" I said, "Yep. All six of 'em for $3.99. What y'all think, I'm a fool? I've seen *King Kong*, the old one and the new one. I've seen *Planet of the Apes*, *The Rise of the Apes*, *War of the Planet of the Apes*, *Dawn of the Planet of the Apes*, *Battle for the Planet of the Apes*, *Escape from the Planet of the Apes*, *Return of the Apes*, and *Kong: Skull Island*. I'm not going to spend eighty-five dollars to watch another monkey."

Everyone has their strengths and weakness. My weakness is simple – I often don't remember people's names, though this inability is not due to a memory problem. Some people simply bear names that are unpronounceable.

You know your last name is rough when you hand your ID over to a cop, and they look at it and say, "Mr. Joe Ka… Ka… Sir, how do you pronounce your last name?" You should change your entire name if someone asks you to spell out your name after pronouncing it. Then, you start spelling it out slowly: "A as in Adam. E as in Eve. P as in Pussy. M as in Monkey…"

Has anyone also noticed that police officers and most military personnel often have a long last name on their name tag?

The ones that annoy me the most are people with difficult names who become belligerent when you don't pronounce their name correctly.

I used to be a supervisor at an M Mart grocery store. One of my employees – man, this dude was from Pakistan or somewhere, I don't know. He had a disastrous first name, and his last name was even worse. Since no one could accurately pronounce his name, we just called him by the first three letters of his last name, Aby. But every time we called him that, he would get mad and pronounce his name completely.

One morning, I was inspecting the store when I bumped into a trash can that was full. So, I called Mr. Aby to ask him why it hadn't been emptied. When he arrived, the first thing that came out of his mouth was, "My name is not Aby. My name is Abynistanm—"

I interrupted him before he could finish, saying, "Sir, when you finish pronouncing your last name, can you take out this trash, please?"

When will Jehovah's Witnesses stop coming to our house? My roommate has been converted to Islam sixteen times, and they're still knocking on our door, trying to give him the same paper every day. That's like Stephen King handing out the same book every year. They knocked on my door the other day, and the first thing I said to them was "Salaam alaikum," and this stubborn lady in a skirt still handed me the book. Because she was nice and looked decent, I accepted the book from her. When I looked at the cover, I said, "Ma'am, ain't this the same book y'all gave me yesterday?"

The lady replied, "No, this one is different. The one I gave you yesterday says, 'God loves you.' This one says, 'Jehovah loves you.'"

In my mind, I wondered, *What the hell is the difference?*

We do strange things in America. And Americans behave this way for two reasons: we either want attention, or we want to look tough. For instance, America is the only country in the world where the Commander in Chief of the Armed Forces signs a bill into law, but doesn't know what the hell goes into the bill. I'll discuss politics later in the book.

One of the main causes of traffic jams on the beltway in any state in America are car accidents. But I've noticed that it's not the accident itself that causes the traffic jam; rather, it is the rubbernecking drivers who are slowing down to watch the accident scene. If state governments could accept the fact that people are naturally inclined to watch strange things, I believe it would help them a lot.

Look at Dubai, for example. In the past, not too many people visited Dubai. But today, if you haven't visited Dubai, you haven't lived. That's because Dubai has some weird and luxurious buildings, and people enjoy looking at strange things.

Imagine if every state government in America decided to buy and use exotic cars, like Lamborghinis and Ferraris, as patrol cars for police officers. If that were the case, it is doubtful that anyone would hate it when cops showed up.

Any random dude in the hood could just walk to the Ferrari patrol car, and say: "Excuse me, officer. I just saw three people smoking crack back there, somewhere. I don't remember the name of the street, but I can take you there if you let me inside your car."

The officer would reply, "Thanks, I got a GPS."

Have you noticed how most police officers like to scare people away with statements like, "Do you want a ride in the back seat?" or "Do you want a ride downtown?" In other words, those two questions mean: "Do you want to get arrested?" But in this scenario, they wouldn't work with anyone. I mean, that's the last question you'd want to ask a person in the hood, if you were a police officer and you happened to be driving a Rolls-Royce Phantom.

Speaking of the hood, why is it that every time you meet a new girl from the hood, the next day is somehow always her birthday?

I dated a girl a while ago, and she celebrated her birthday twice in one week. I met her at a shoe store, and she immediately told me, "My birthday is tomorrow," which was on that Saturday. So, I wished her happy birthday, took her out the next day, and we had a good time. On Sunday, the day after her birthday, I called her. I guess she didn't save my number, or something. She answered the phone.

"Hey, what's up?" I asked.

"Hey."

"What are you doing today?"

"Nothing. You?"

"Nothing. I was just about to do laundry when I decided to call you." I replied.

"Cool, cool. You know tomorrow is my birthday, right?"

"Your birthday, or your sister's birthday?"

"No… my birthday."

"Alright, baby. Let me get something straight. Is tomorrow the day you were born, or the day you were born again?"

"The day I was born. Why?"

"What are you, an alien or something?" I retorted.

She was confused, just like I was. She replied, "Who is this?"

I lied to her. I said, "John."

"Which John?" she replied.

"John the Baptist."

She said, "Hey, John, I have a birthday wish. Do you want to know what it is?"

I hung up before the witch could request my

head. After that conversation, I saved her number on my phone as "The Queen of All Liars."

America is the land of the brave. Yet, you would be surprised to hear of the kind of things that scare Americans, such as stink bugs, spiders, boogie men, zombies, clowns, and mice. Even though we know some of these are fictional characters from movies, we are still scared of them.

How is George Bush a football fan, yet he can't catch a shoe thrown ten feet away from him? But he can sure duck, though. Man... he ducked that shoe so fast, the Secret Service agents around him thought they were watching Neo in *The Matrix*.

There are so many mysteries in the world that mystify me. There are three that baffle me the most.

The first one is a phenomenon without a name, as far as I'm concerned; and even if it does, I don't want to know it. I call it "motion dilation."

Some of you must have experienced it before. It's what happens after your car stops completely at a red light. For no apparent reason, you looked at the other car beside you and thought your car was backing up. Out of fear, you apply more force to the break, but you see your car is still moving. Just as you are about to have a heart attack, you then realize it isn't your car that's moving; it's the stupid car you were paying attention to that was.

The second one is called a "déjà vu." I don't know the language from which "déjà vu" originated, but I call that shit "paranormal activity." From its name alone, anybody could tell that something isn't right.

How the heck did the same exact occurrence that happened ten years ago repeat itself again in the present, in the same exact way?

The first time I experienced a déjà vu, it was as though I were under hypnosis. It happened on the wrong day, at the wrong place, and at the wrong time. So much so that I couldn't share the experience with the person I was with.

I was on a first date that evening at Hooters, having a good time. It was a nice restaurant with good food, and my girl was looking gorgeous – everything was going fine. For the record, I swear that was my first time at that restaurant. Seriously, I had never been there before. So, my girl and I were having a good time, until one of the servers came along and asked, "You guys need anything?" I was the first to look up, and somehow, my eyes went directly towards her waist, and I stared at it for a good three seconds. Don't blame me; I was just experiencing déjà vu, caused by this half-naked woman.

"No thanks, we're good," my date replied.

I don't know from where that woman popped out. I didn't know who she was. I just knew that I had seen her before, standing in front of me in that same way and asking me that same question. If I had been with my friend, Dave, I would have said, "Yo, Dave, it seems as if I've seen that big-ass girl before." But I was on a date. How do you tell the woman you are dating something like that? So, when the time came for me to explain, I had to make up a story. We were in the middle of a conversation, and out of the blue, my girl asked, "So... do you know her?"

"I'm sorry—do I know who?"

"The server you were staring at earlier. Do you know her?"

"Oh, Sister Rose. She used to be one of our church members before she backslid."

The third one is perhaps the most inexplicable occurrence in the universe. How does a person work all day and then go to bed at night, thinking they are about to get some rest, only to find themselves on a battlefield fighting aliens as soon as they lay their head on the pillow? They're dreaming, and think, "I'm not even in the military. What the hell am I doing in Afghanistan?"

I know I'm not the only one who flies in my dreams. Some of you do, or you're just pretending you don't. The first time I heard the song "I Believe I Can Fly" by R. Kelly, I thought, "This brother needs to stop smoking crack", because the only place where any human can ever fly is in their dreams. It's cool to fly in your dreams. What is not cool is when a grown-ass man tries to fly in real life. Folks, forget about *Batman* and *Superman*. I've been flying in my dreams before airplanes were invented.

My dreams are crazy. I mean, if every person's dream happens to come true one day, nobody on earth will still be greater than I am. If you think your dreams are wild, wait until you hear mine. I was the first human to walk on the moon. In my dreams.

The first time I got behind the wheel of a car, my mother was sitting next to me, thinking she was about to teach me how to drive. To her surprise, when we got to the parking lot, I drove her new Cadillac like a professional. She was amazed. She asked me, "Who taught you how to drive?"

"You," I replied.

With slight confusion on her face, she looked at me and said, "When?"

"In my dream."

My mum is hilarious. She is the only one who

cashes her check at the bank, and then deposits the money in her bra. The funniest part is that, every time we ask her for money, she'll write a check before taking the money from her bra. She claims, "I do it to keep track of my money." I would reply, "Mum, what is this – the *Bra* of America?"

One singer said, "Women are a mystery that men can't understand." I couldn't agree more. Ladies, there are a lot of things that you do that men will never understand. For instance, how the heck do you wear makeup to the gym? Why do you wear short skirts to church? And what the hell is inside that handbag you carry with you everywhere you go?

Fellas, have you mistakenly opened your wife or girlfriend's bag, and it felt as if you had mistakenly opened a mechanic's toolbox? And then they'll ask you a question that will make you feel like you're a creepy stranger: "Why are you looking inside my bag?"

I once looked inside my girlfriend's bag, and

the only thing I recognized was a screwdriver. I was like, "Baby, why do you have a screwdriver inside your bag?"

She asked me that somewhat accusatory question, as if her bag contained a spell within that must not be unearthed. When I didn't reply, she continued: "You'll find out on the day I catch your ass cheating on me." Since then, I have been curious to know what is inside every woman's bag.

The following week, I went to my cousin's house for a family reunion, and saw my ten-year-old niece carrying a little bag over her shoulder. I requested, "Kim, let me see what's inside your bag." When she handed me the little pink bag, I opened it and saw a lipstick, a candy... and a hotdog. After that, I became even more curious to see what every woman in the house had inside their bags. The next one I could lay my hands on belonged to my grandma. I opened it, and it was as if I had opened a forbidden box. I found lottery tickets, a lipstick, a crab leg, a Bible, a Taser, and a dildo. Before I could close the bag, my grandma walked in and caught me with it. I looked at her, she looked at me, I looked at her, she looked at me, and then she asked me that same question: "Why're you looking inside my bag?"

I said, "Oh, hell no. I'm never ever going to look inside any woman's bag ever again."

If I were to ask people who the most famous actor of all time is, I'm sure many would answer incorrectly. Yet, you know him. In fact, you know him very well. Some of you even have his picture in your house right now. Ladies and gentlemen, that man whose picture hangs on the wall in your bedroom is not Jesus—his name is Robert Powell. I told my mum this a million times, but she won't listen. Every day before she leaves the house, she'll go to where she has hung Powell's picture, and say, "Jesus, please keep this house safe in my absence. Don't let me come back and see my house on fire. And keep those thugs and thieves off my property. I don't like them. Thank you, Jesus," as though Jesus Christ worked for ADT.

One morning, before leaving for work, I took the picture off the wall and hid it. She didn't notice it was missing when she returned home from work that day, because the only time she prays to Jesus is when she's heading out of the house. When she's at home, she's Jesus.

As she was about to go to work the next morning, she decided to pray to her house insurance, Jesus, as per usual. I was in my room when I heard a heavy knock on the door. As soon as I heard her voice, I knew exactly what was going on, but pretended as though I hadn't had a clue. I opened the door hurriedly and said, "Mum, what happened? Is the house on fire?"

She slapped me, before saying, "My house will never be on fire, in Jesus's name. Where is my picture?"

"Your picture is on Instagram, mum," I replied while still reeling from the slap I had just received. She slapped me again, and then asked the right question: "Where is my Jesus picture?"

"I took it off the wall."

"Why did you remove Jesus's picture from my wall?"

"Mum, that ain't no Jesus. Man...I told you that already." I replied.

"Oh boy, so now you want to tell me what Jesus looks like. I've been praying to him since before I gave birth to you."

"You've been praying to Powell before you gave birth to me."

"Powell! Is that Jesus's last name?"

"No. That's Robert's last name. That's the name of the actor you've been referring to as Jesus."

"Damn, he looks just like Jesus," my mum exclaimed as she walked away. "Those eyes! He doesn't look like he's one of us."

Let's talk about some delightful stuff for a moment, before we continue.

How in the world did Jeff Bozo pass Bill Gates in wealth? I've noticed something about rich people. It seems as if the people who have big money lack big ideas, while the people who have great ideas lack money. Come to think of it—if money could change the world, the rich would have done it by now, right? Don't get me wrong; we've traveled a long way since we began using our brains. Nevertheless, if you pay close attention, you'll realize that the world is still far behind. And this little change that the world desperately needs, just happens to be in the heads of people like me and you.

How hard is it for car manufacturers to create a car that can jump-start itself with a push of a button, and refill its own break, washer, and antifreeze fluids? Just like ruminant animals, all the car would require is an extra battery and extra storage for its fluids.

Did you know that it was possible to design a car that could inflate any of its four tires with the push of a button? How many of you would prefer to sacrifice a little trunk space for a bigger fuel tank? I could even go further by saying that it's possible to have technology in a car that can perform an oil change. But I guess Jiffy Lube wouldn't like that idea. And that's one of the problems the world is facing today. Great ideas do not see the light of day, because *someone* thinks they might lose a profit. Of course, this is not always the case. For instance, when Tesla cars—and electric cars, in general—were made, some people said this would mark the beginning of the end for oil companies. "Gas stations will no longer exist," they said. Electric cars have now been around for almost a decade, and oil companies are still in business. The logic is simple –big money does not generate big ideas; rather, big ideas generate big money. So, poor people are not so poor, after all. Even though we don't have big money, we have big ideas—most of which are referred to as "infamous ideas." But then, when these so-called geniuses release their "ingenious ideas," some of them will make you wonder if the human brain has stopped evolving.

Can someone tell me what in the world they do on Google+? Do any of you have Google+ accounts? Do you know *anyone* who has a Google Plus account? But to the person who came up with the concept, Google+ was an ingenious idea. Don't get me wrong; I'm not saying this thing doesn't work—most of us have an account, but we didn't directly or intentionally sign up for it. We got registered because we already had a Google account. All that I'm trying to say is that a company who runs almost eighty percent of the internet could have come up with better social networking ideas.

In 2010, the founder of Facebook, Mark Zuckerberg, reportedly donated a whopping hundred million dollars to Newark public schools. Some years later, rumors spread that the school's management couldn't account for what they had done with the money. Why am I telling you this? What if—instead of donating the money—Facebook had started an online reality game, where fifty-dollar bills totaling a hundred million dollars were hidden in secret places, like a treasure island? People could try to find money in large places, and walk around like in Grand Theft Auto games. They could interact with each other with open headphones ("open" as in, if you put on the headphones, you can hear everything around you like you would in real life). Players would have to link their bank card to their Facebook account to receive the money they had found, like Cash App. By now, I believe the online Facebook marketplace would have surpassed eBay.

If the amount hidden in the Facebook treasure island reality game were the same amount Mark Zuckerberg had donated in 2012, which amounted to five hundred million dollars, for the record, by now, the online Facebook market would have surpassed Amazon.

Those of you who live in America have seen something like this in politics. It's called a stimulus package. That's when the President of the United States gives free money to working Americans, either through tax reduction or through a check.

If Google had set a date once every month to give out twenty dollars each to the first forty thousand people who logged into Google+ after its launch, and shared a post and a picture, Google+ would have surpassed Instagram and

Twitter in total number of active users by now. That day of the month would be no different to Black Friday.

Let me touch on another aspect before I resume writing jokes. If you live in America, let me ask you this question: when was the last time you visited Arby's, or Starbucks? I'm sure you've heard those names, even if you've never visited. Do you know that most people who go to Starbucks daily, go there only to use the free wi-fi? It's only after a while, when they are hungry or thirsty, that they'll order something to eat or drink.

I'm a regular Starbucks and Panera Bread customer. It's the free wi-fi and charging outlets that attract me to my favorite food places, in the same way the fifty-cent ice cream cone and a dollar McChicken brings thousands of people to Burger King and McDonald's every day. Okay, a word to the wise is enough—let's get back to jokes.

Who the hell came up with the idea of vehicle state inspection? That's what happens after you've just bought a car – the state requires you to take it to a state-licensed mechanic for a safety checkup before you are issued a license plate. The actual inspection is not what I consider annoying – even though it is, but I'll get to that very soon. What annoys me most is the reason for the inspection. The state wants to ensure that every car on the road is safe—that's cool. Ain't nothing wrong with safety. But why the hell did you give me a thirty-day temporary tag to drive the car around if you are not so sure the car is safe to be on the road? And for those of you who live in America, please don't tell me you're given the temporary tag so you can have enough time to get the car to the inspection station. Please, don't give me that excuse. That's not reasonable. What if I ran over your grandmother on my way to the inspection station because my breaks didn't work properly?

Earlier, I mentioned how I thought the inspection itself was also annoying. It's preposterous how you get to the inspection station, and the mechanic informs you that your car failed inspection because of things like "faulty door handle," "alignment," "cracked side-view mirror", etc. Now, tell me –how many times have you turned on the news and heard that a faulty door handle caused an accident on the road? Have you ever read in a newspaper of a car flipping over on the beltway because the car alignment was not balanced? What's even more heartbreaking is when the mechanic tells you it will cost two thousand dollars to fix a car you had bought for fifteen hundred dollars at an auction. HELL NO! SCAMMERS!

It's like with the lottery, when the public is informed that the jackpot is five hundred million dollars. When a winner comes forward to claim the money and dare to ask for a lump-sum payment, they are then told that cash-out would be two hundred million dollars before taxes. So, what in the world happened to the other three hundred million, bro? Then, of course, the company will tell you that you can get the entire amount only if you are willing to take it in instalments over a period of twenty years or so. Really?

As though we don't know how interest works? Depending on a bank's interest rate, if you deposit three hundred million dollars in a five percent interest rate savings account over the span of 20 years, your three hundred million dollars would have accumulated to around a hundred and eighty million dollars in interest. So, after twenty years, bro, who is going to take home the interest...? Exactly! Scammers!

The next thing I will discuss should be listed among the Seven Wonders of the World. Motion sensors are the result of a beautiful technological idea. But then, they started to appear in restrooms.

It's cool when the door automatically opens as a person is approaching it. It's cool when the light automatically turns on when you enter a restroom. What is not cool is when the toilet starts flushing when someone is taking a shit. Guys, that is not cool at all.

After all the constant flushing that took place while you were taking a shit, you'd expect a toilet like that to flush as soon as you stand up, right? Nope. With these toilets, you must lean over and wave your hand in front of the sensor multiple times before it flushes. After you are done with that fiasco, it's time to wash your hands, and the saga continues. To get the hand soap dispenser to work, you have to wave at the sensor. To get the tap water running, you must wave at the sink. And finally, to get a tissue paper to clean your hand, you must wave at the tissue dispenser.

Has the tissue paper in a dispenser ever taken so long to come out that you literally had to drag the sheet out of it? Or have you ever stayed in a restroom for so long while taking a shit, that the light automatically turned off, leaving you in total darkness? The bottom line is: motion sensors are cool, but not in a restroom.

I'm going to touch on one more thing, and I'll follow it up with a story. If you drive a sedan, you must have noticed those annoying long bricks that are placed at the end of a parking space, designed to stop you from running your

49

car into the building. Some of those bricks are so high that if you mistakenly drive your front bumper over them and decide to back up a little, you'll end up hearing the noise of the brick tearing apart your bumper. Now, the question I have is, who created those ugly bricks? Please don't tell me that an intelligent designer did. Sometimes, there are things we as humans do that make me want to go to the zoo, and apologize to the apes. Humans lock them up, as though apes can't make good decisions on their own. In some areas, though, monkeys are much wiser than some humans. For instance, under no circumstances will a chimp jump inside a tiger's lair, not even to pick up a banana. That said, some years ago in New York City, a moron—one of us, a human—intentionally jumped inside a tiger's lair to pet it. Even a baboon, the dumbest of all monkeys, wouldn't behave that way.

The dumbest human behavior is when we use age as an excuse for our unreasonable behavior.

There was a junior high school behind my

former apartment in Maryland. Behind the apartments, there is a back road between some houses that lead to the school. When students would get off the bus, they had the habit of walking in the middle of that road.

I was driving on it one afternoon, and there were a bunch of students in the middle of the road. I honked my horn several times, but they wouldn't get out of the way. So, I rolled down my window and told them to move.

A lady passing by heard me and got offended, and her excuse was even more stupid than a bunch of teenagers walking in the middle of the road. She said, "Sir, they are just kids!"

'Kids'? Kids, my ass! I have a Chihuahua; his name is Crispy. He will be fourteen months this October. Crispy will never, even when he's by himself, walk in the middle of the damned road. Are you telling me a bunch of humans who can operate an iPhone 8 don't know the difference between a sidewalk and a road?

I was smart like a rat when I was younger. When

I was in eighth grade, my mum was so stingy that we had to lie to get money from her.

A girl in my class had died, and we were asked by the school to bring a donation for her family the next day. When I got home, I told my mum about it, and she gave me ten dollars to donate. I was amazed. Ten dollars was a lot of money back in 1995.

Two days later, I came back from school looking all dejected. My mum came back from work that evening, saw me looking sad, and asked what had happened. I replied with a gloomy voice, "My math teacher at school died."

"Which one, the light-skinned one?" My mum replied.

I didn't know who the light-skinned one was, but I'm quick on my feet. So, I said, while crying like a baby, "Yeah, the short, light-skinned one with long hair."

My mum was all sympathetic, caressing me, hugging me, and rubbing my back. While she was in that remorseful mood, I told her the school had asked us to bring a donation for the deceased's family.

Can you guess how much money she gave me the next day to donate? Fifteen dollars. I thought, "Holy Christ, this thing works!"

Two days later, my mum came home early because our neighbor had called her and told her I wouldn't stop crying after I'd come back from school. As soon as she entered the house, she went straight to my room and found me sitting on the floor, crying. She asked, "What happened?"

I didn't say a word. I just kept on crying. My mum was like, "Did you hear me...? I said, what happened?"

With a deep, shaking voice, I replied, "Five teachers at my school died..."

"Including your math teacher?"

"Yeah," I replied. That's where I messed up. I forgot I had used my math teacher's death to collect some money days ago.

She'd just caught me red-handed in a lie. My mum was smart too, so she decided to be sarcastic with her response. She said, "Who's your math teacher, Lazarus?"

If I had been reading the Bible, I would have known who Lazarus was, and by then realized the jig was up. But I was young and dumb. So, the moment she brought up the name Lazarus, I made up another story. In a fake-crying voice, I replied, "Yeah, my math teacher, Lazarus. The tall, dark-skinned one with short hair."

My mum was surprised to discover how greedy I was. She stood up from the couch and said, "Put on your clothes."

"Mum, where are we going?" I asked.

With a soft, yet wild voice, my mum replied, "Don't call me Mum. Call me Jesus."

When my mum tells you to do something, you do it without argument. So, I rephrased the question. Instead of calling her "mum", I obeyed and said, "Jesus, where're we going?"

"To your school."

"What are we going to do there?"

With that same gentle, yet wild voice, she replied, "Boy, I'm going to raise up Lazarus from the dead today."

"Jesus, Lazarus has been dead for a couple of days. I'm sure by now, his body has probably been buried."

My mum replied with yet another sarcastic remark, letting me know that, had I read the Bible, I would have known the jig was up. She said, *"I'm the resurrection and the life. He that believeth in me, though he were dead, yet shall he live."*

We got in the car, and my legs were shaking. As soon as my mum pulled out of the driveway, she said something implying I was dead meat. She said it with that same soft, yet wild voice, while looking me straight in the eye: "Boy, when I raise Lazarus up today—*oh*, he'd better have my fifteen dollars, or else *somebody* is going to take his place."

I love my mum. The fear of my mum is the beginning of wisdom. If you had lived in our house when I was young, you would know that my mum only calls us once, but twice do we hear her voice.

My mum and I were watching a football

game one evening in the living room when a commercial came on. I don't know who had come up with its concept, but it was funny as hell. The commercial was about barbecue. A man sitting next to his mother said: "This barbecue tastes so good it will make you wanna slap yo mama." He then went on and slapped her.

I wanted to laugh, but inexplicably glanced over in the direction of where my mum was seated, and she had been staring at me. She looked at me dead in the eyes. To appease her, I quickly blurted out, "Mum, I don't even like barbecue."

"I didn't ask you," she retorted. From the way she said it, I thought she was cool with the commercial, so I asked if I could laugh. But then she said, "Sure, why not? But after you're done laughing, why don't you go outside and dig your grave?"

So, here's the story I said I would relate. Ask yourself this question: what's the most important thing in life? In my opinion, the correct answer is happiness. If you take happiness out of anything in life, that thing will no longer make sense. And true happiness comes when you achieve something great, and you are satisfied with it.

This story is about a blind man, Coare, and his sighted guard, Pen. They both live on a planet without light.

Every time, the temple's bell across the street would ring, Coare would step outside his house and wait for Pen to help him navigate his way to the temple. Pen was always happy to help Coare. He saw it as an honor.

He was never late. As soon as he would hear the bell ringing, he would make his way to Coare's house in a hurry. In return, Coare would share his income with Pen. This went on for a long time.

One day, on their way to the temple and after Coare had just finished sharing his money with Pen, a meteorite crashed into the planet with a huge flash of light visible from twenty miles away. Coare stopped and looked at the meteorite as it was descending towards the planet.

Surprised, he looked at Pen and exclaimed, "I can see!" Pen asked, "How?"

"I just saw something huge fly across the sky. Did you see it?" Coare replied.

"That's not possible. How could any of us see something on this dark planet?"

The meteorite caused a fire after it had landed, and was still visible from many miles away. Coare could see it, but Pen could not. It had turned out that Coare wasn't blind, after all; he had only assumed he was blind because he couldn't see anything due to the total darkness that loomed in his planet. Pen, on the other hand, was blind, but he had thought the reason he couldn't see anything was because the planet was too dark.

All this while, Pen had been helping Coare get to the temple safely—by faith, not by sight. Pen had thought Coare had known this, which was why Pen had always considered helping him to be an honor.

I'm relating this story to you because I have been searching for happiness my entire life. Whenever I see people accomplish great things in life, I wonder how they did it. I want to be successful. I want to do great things in life. But I don't know how, or where to start.

One day, an LA Fitness member gave me a three-day workout pass for their gym. I called the gym that afternoon to ask about their boot camp, and I was told there was one coming up at 7 a.m. the following day, which was then a Saturday.

That Saturday morning, I went to the indoor basketball court in the gym, and there were twenty or so people there, waiting. We didn't know who the personal trainer was, but we were told at the front desk that he was running late because his wife had just delivered their baby that morning. While we were all getting ready for the session, a guy walked onto the court, dressed in tight leggings with his shirt tucked in, long socks up to his calves, and white sneakers. He turned on the music, and started giving us instructions.

First, our group started with a dramatic set of 100 pushups, followed by 150 suicides. There was no break in between. The moment we completed one move, we had to start the next one. Everyone was sweating horribly. I had never seen a workout like that in my life. There were people on the floor who couldn't even move anymore. This guy was screaming at the top of his lungs, louder than the radio he had on, and calling out for stunts, acrobatic moves, and summersaults. After fifteen minutes, everybody was lying on the floor, sweating.

We were all getting ready to start a ridiculous set of 500 kangaroo jumps, when another guy walked in. He was dressed in a black Nike workout outfit with the words "personal trainer" written on the back of his hoodie. He turned off the radio and said, "What the hell is going on here?" before addressing his attention to the guy who had been training us for about fifteen minutes, "Pollo, what are you doing here, man?" Two other guys from the gym also came in, and all three men walked Pollo out.

When the guy dressed in black came back, most of us were still lying on the floor, trying to catch our breath, while others who were more fit were seated. He picked up the mic and apologized for being late. Then, he introduced himself as our personal trainer.

One lady who was overweight and dying on the floor said, "What? Hold on. If you are the personal trainer, who the hell was the guy training us earlier?"

He replied, "Guys, I apologize for the misunderstanding. That guy from earlier is not your personal trainer. He's not even supposed to be here. His nickname is Pollo. He just escaped from a psychiatric hospital in the area."

All of us were like, "Hell no..." Another fat lady in the crowd who was just recovering said, "Excuse me, sir—what is a kangaroo jump?"

The personal trainer was surprised.

"Y'all did Kangaroo jumps?"

Somebody else answered, "No, but we were about to. That's what we were getting ready to do when you entered."

The trainer said, "Oh, my God… Guys, I'm very sorry. You are not supposed to do kangaroo jumps at all. That's the worst training in the Navy SEALs recruiting process. None of you here will last twenty seconds if you start it." One of the fat ladies started crying.

This is what I learned that day: belief and courage. Although the crazy guy wasn't a personal trainer, he stepped forward and acted like one. In his own unique way, he even exceeded what a qualified trainer could do (except for the kangaroo jumps). We asked the real personal trainer to demonstrate a kangaroo jump after he finished our training session. A kangaroo jump is when you carry another person the same size as you on your back or arm, and run a mile or perform fifty suicides non-stop.

On the second day of the boot camp, one of the ladies who almost had a seizure from the day before went straight to the trainer after entering the gym and asked, "Are you the real trainer for this session?"

"Yes, ma'am," the trainer replied.

The lady said, "*Mm-hmm*. Baby, I got to see some ID. Ain't nobody here doing kangaroo jumps today. *Uh-uh*, not today."

Enough with the kangaroos. As I was saying, that crazy Pollo guy showed me the first step towards success. He taught me that its greatest secret is that it is linked to courage and belief in one's self.

Fear lives in the heart of humans. Some people have it in a large amount, while others have little of it. No human can completely rid themselves of fear. Yet, we can eliminate it in many if not most aspects of our lives, by taking a bold step.

Alright, let me crack you up a little. Fellas, please, please, and please—I'm gonna say it one more time. Fellas, please. If a lady pulls up in a Porsche or an S550 AMG, and you happen to be driving a Honda—I don't care what make and model your Honda is, 2000, 2018, or 2024; I don't care!—please remember that a Honda is a

Honda. Do *not* try to get her number. Why? The answer is simple: SHE WON'T GIVE IT TO YOU.

Guys, you don't have to embarrass yourself. If you see a girl driving a nice, expensive car, trust me when I say that she has a boyfriend. And if she doesn't, she's got a vibrator with which she's satisfied. See, I already knew this; but my stupid friend, Dave, always likes to embarrass himself. What I don't appreciate is when he forces me to do stuff I don't want to do.

One time, Dave and I had just left a bowling joint on a Saturday evening in Dave's Honda Civic. He was driving. I was chilling in the front passenger seat. While I was browsing the web on my phone, I heard him say, "I'm gonna race this Bentley."

I looked up, and a white fully-tinted Bentley GT Continental was right in front of us at the red light. When the light turned green, Dave pulled up alongside the driver's side of the Bentley and signaled to its driver that he wanted to race. The window on the driver's side slowly rolled halfway down, and we saw this sexy, light-skinned woman sitting in the driver's seat. I guess she was confused as to what Dave was trying to signal. A few moments later, she rolled up her window, and made a left turn into the parking lot of a Shoppers grocery store. And of course, my stupid-ass friend, Dave, also made a left turn and followed her right into the parking lot. She parked, and we parked not too far from where her car was, with seven or so parking spaces were between us. I looked at Dave, with an expression on my face that begged the question, "What the hell are you doing, bro?"

Dave instinctively replied, "You wanna go get her number?"

"Dude, she's driving a Bentley."

"So what? She's driving a car, and we're driving a car, too," Dave argued.

"No, Dave, there's a huge difference between a Bentley and a Civic. One single tire on that Bentley can buy your Honda. Plus, Dave, you know I have a girlfriend."

"You're scared, man."

"I'm not interested in the girl. But just so you know—I'm not scared. I'm gonna go to her car and get her number." That was the plan. I came out of our Honda, walked to the Bentley, and knocked on the driver's side window.

When no one responded, I knocked on the window a second time. This time, when the window came down, it came *a-a-a-ll* the way down.

Remember when I mentioned that we saw a sexy, light-skinned lady driving the Bentley when she rolled down her window halfway? Well, what Dave and I didn't know was that there was a guy sitting in the front passenger seat of the Bentley. Now, fellas, why is it that when your girlfriend is driving, and y'all riding in the front passenger seat, you like to roll the seat back and relax for no *fucking* reason? We didn't see the idiot because his seat was rolled back, as he relaxed while his girlfriend was driving.

As soon as I bent over to start a conversation with this chick, from my peripheral vision, I saw this big, muscular dude relaxing in the front passenger seat. He and the light-skinned lady stared at me immediately. I swear, I almost peed in my pants. I mean, the girl was staring directly at me, and I couldn't say a word.

Suddenly, the dude said impatiently, "WHAT?"

But, as you know, I'm quick on my feet and smart like a monkey, so I made up a story right then and there. I replied, "Ma'am, have you surrendered your life to Jesus? I'm one of Jehovah's Witnesses going from car to car, preaching the gospel of Jesus."

I had messed up again, and the dude caught me red-handed. I suck at making up stories on the fly. He replied, "Jehovah's Witnesses don't believe in going around preaching the gospel of Jesus. What kind of Jehovah's Witness are you?"

"Bro, Jehovah's Witness these days—you'd be surprised in whom they believe, especially the ones I belong to. We believe in everything: Jesus, Buddha, Mohamed, Allah, Illuminati—sir, will you be interested in reading one of our books?"

Neither of them said a word. They just kept staring at me. So, I did myself a favor by ending the painful conversation, and walking away.

When I got back inside the Civic, Dave said, "What took you so long? Did you get her number?"

At first, I stayed quiet while I looked at him. If he had known how mad I was, he would have just started the car and kept on going. But I wanted him to experience what he had just put me through. So, I told him the lady wouldn't give me her number, and that she insisted on talking to the cute guy driving the Honda instead.

Dave was happy. "She called me 'cute'?" he asked.

"Yeah," I replied.

For the record, Dave is ugly as shit. I mean, there's no secret about it. I say it to his face all the time.

He said, "Stop playing, man. She didn't say that."

"I swear, Dave. She said she won't leave the parking lot unless she talks to you."

As soon as I said that, Dave jumped out of the car, and ran towards the Bentley like a deer crossing the beltway.

I was sitting in the car, watching his dumb ass through the windshield glass. For some reason, when he got to the Bentley, he did the same thing I did. First, he knocked on the window on the driver's side, and when the window rolled down, he bent over to talk to the lady in the driver's seat. I couldn't hear what they were saying, but I knew it must have been pure hell for Dave.

A few seconds later, he returned to the car looking like a homeless cat. He stared at me for a second, before he started the engine.

I asked, "Dave, what happened? Did you get the number?"

He didn't say a word. He just kept on driving.

Days later, when his anger had died down, we had a chance to talk about what had happened.

"In my mind, I was like, *Holy...shit.* I was confused. I was smiling, but the girl wasn't smiling. That was when I realized your dumb ass had set me up. The dude looked me dead in the eye before he asked with a deep voice, 'What do you want, man?' Bro, I didn't know why I thought of Geico at that moment, but it was all I could think of. I said, 'Ma'am, if you give me five minutes to get something from my car, I can show you how fifteen minutes can save you fifteen percent or more on car insurance.'"

Ladies and gentlemen, there are only two people in this world who have told you the truth: Jesus and me. Every other person has only tried.

Ladies, don't let anyone deceive you. There are only three things in life that motivate a man: God, money, and women. The book of Ecclesiastes touches on this regarding money, when the writer said, "Money answers all things." Thus, if you are reading this book, and you are trying to be all smart and pretentious about what I claimed motivates a man, cut it. You ain't smarter than the Bible.

The second one is deep, but don't worry—I'll break it down for you. You've likely heard the expression, "Money makes the world go round." Well, whoever made that statement was wrong because, it is in fact women and gravity that make the world go round. Let me be completely honest. Ladies, men wouldn't care about *anything* in this world if it weren't for you. You are the reason we hustle. You are the reason we swag. You are the reason we go to the gym. You are the reason we want a Ferrari. You are the reason we wear Versace and Gucci belts. You are the reason we wear bling-bling. And yes—ladies, you are the reason we use Viagra. If all the women in the world were to suddenly disappear right now, 99.9% percent of men would not go to the club tonight.

Mercedes-Benz, Ferrari, Gucci, Bentley, and all these exotic companies would go out of business. The gym would lose the membership of their male clients. Let's be honest ladies, no man is interested in having a six-pack. Men like to eat. That's what we like to do. None of us wants a six-pack; we only do it for you. Even God knew how nonsensical the world would be if women were not around; that's why he quickly created

Eve, before Adam started messing with the female monkeys in the garden. I mean, read the Bible closely. Adam wasn't alone in the garden. God was always there with him. So, if a helper was what Adam truly needed, why didn't God just create another man to help him? Nope. God understood that nothing can replace the pussy. Not an apple, not a cute garden, not a waterfall, not even God Himself.

Men were clueless about life, until women came along and started telling us what they liked. They told us they liked long beards, so now every dude wants a long beard. They told us they liked six-packs, so now every man wants a six-pack. They told us they liked big arms, so guess what—every man now wants big arms.

You will be surprised to learn that letting your pants sag is not a fashion trend. Sagging actually started because a lady said something like, "Women like to see a clean man's boxers above his belt." That was how sagging started.

I thought NASA were the only ones going around looking for aliens, until I met my ex.

Ladies, let me explain something to you. Looking for a good man on earth is like NASA looking for aliens on the moon. Men are men, and none of us are right.

A while ago, I was talking to this woman and she was trying to make her man seem like he was different from the rest of us.

"My man is different. He doesn't eat greasy food. He's classy. He doesn't look at other girls. He's different." she claimed.

I replied, "Baby girl, how much do you make in a year?"

"Not too much, just a little over eighty thousand."

I said, "Girl, your man *ain't* different. Your man is a player. Let me tell you something, baby. Men—including your man—have two brains. One is inside our skull, and the other one is between our legs. Don't get me wrong; some men have principles. However, I don't know what your man has told you about himself, but the truth is men love one thing in this world more than anything else God has created: a good-looking woman, with a good-looking ass and good-looking titties. Period. Such a woman is the reason men go to the gym and lift weights or why we dress to impress. She's also why we get nice haircuts, want a six-pack, drive a Benz, and lastly, the reason men use Viagra.

If you don't get it, you don't get it.

Next, I'm going to take you on a tour of every country I've been to so far.

Let me start with Canada. When will Canadian immigration officials stop making Canada seem like it's a twenty-hour flight away from America?

One sunny afternoon in Minnesota, I was hiking when a cop stopped my bike. The officer said, "Sir, what is the purpose of your visit to Canada?"

I was confused, because I hadn't realized I just crossed the border from Minnesota into Canada.

"*I'm in Canada?*"

"Yeah. You don't know where you are, sir?" he replied.

That was the question that pissed me off. He said it as though there was a huge wall in the middle of the woods along the border, demarcating Canada from America.

I've also been to the UK. I went there some months ago. The United Kingdom is cool. It's like the United States, except for a few differences. I must confess, I didn't see any kingdom while I was in the "United Kingdom." Folks, they have more ghetto in this so-called kingdom than I've ever seen in the United States.

One of the major differences I noticed between both countries was that most cops in the UK didn't carry firearms. As an American, that amazed me. A UK cop is like a handsome man who lives among millions of prostitutes but doesn't have a dick.

However, I love the way the English speak. Their accent makes them sound like an American who's speaking, while chewing a hot pepper.

I've also been to Mexico. I traveled from Texas to Cancun for a three-day visit. I still don't know why in the world I caught a plane there. I should have caught a cab. That's how close Mexico is to America.

I arrived at Cancun International Airport on a Friday evening. At the arrivals, they checked my bag. I went to another terminal, and they checked my bag a second time. Then, after I thought I was through, they wanted to check my bag a third time. I got mad and refused to let them inspect it. A Mexican airport security official came up to me, and uttered the saddest threat ever to me. He said, "Sir, you *do* understand we can send you back to the United States if you refuse to follow our rules, right?"

I was flabbergasted. Do you know the look that says "WTF" that you give to someone when they ask you a dumb question, like, "Sir, are you a male or a female?" I gave him that look before I went sarcastic on his ass. I replied, "Oh, I should fear going back to America, huh? 'Cause I'm going to lose that good-paying job I have in Cancun? I'm going to lose my health insurance, my 401(k), and that good economy that Mexico is known for, right? *Amigo, please…*"

"*Nantsssssssss ingonyama bagithi Baba. Sithi uhm ingonyama. Siyo Nqoba. Ingonyama nengw' enamabala.*" WHAT'S UP…AFRICANS? The land of the genes, and home of the greats. If you want to be real about it, you can change that to "the land of the genes, and home of the apes." I love Africa. You've got to love it. Africa is the only continent where people have money but still dress like broke people.

I once went to JFK Airport to pick up this brother from Ghana who came to perform at a nightclub in Washington, D.C. When I met him at the arrivals, I said, "Brother, *what you got on, man?*"

He was like, "Brother, this is a dashiki—Africa's finest."

"Bro, a 'dashiki' is what broke people wear in America," I replied.

With his African accent, he said, "No, no, no, brother. I'm not broke. You can ask my entourage. I have a lot of money."

"Then, I'm gonna need y'all to dress like y'all *got* some money," I said to him, as all twenty of them wore the same thing—dashikis.

Let me tell you what happened the first time I visited Nairobi. At first, I was skeptical about going to Africa. But I thought, "What's the worst that could happen when I get there? Get to the Airport and see a K9 officer, walking around with a grown lion? I've seen it before in Dubai." The difference might have been that the lions in Dubai were domesticated, while the ones in Africa likely came straight out of the jungle. Still, I packed my bag and got on the plane.

Man… do you know how long the flight is from New York to Nairobi, Kenya? Seventeen hours. I had never flown for that long before. At one point during the flight, I thought about going to the cockpit to check on the pilot, to make sure he was still in charge of the plane. For those of you who don't know, you gamble your life every time you fly on a plane. I didn't want to sit there thinking I was going to Africa, when, in fact, the plane was going to heaven. When I get to heaven, I want to be able to explain to Jesus how I got there. I don't like surprises.

We are told Bin Laden is dead. Yet there was a guy on board who looked just like him. I kept my eyes on him the entire flight. Everything he did, I copied. When he sneezed, I sneezed. When he stood up, I stood up. When he went to the restroom, I followed him there. Everywhere he went, I followed. I guess he noticed I was following him. Someone was in the bathroom when we got to the lavatory the second time, so both of us had to wait at the door.

I stood behind him while we waited for the person inside to come out. He looked back at me, and said, "Are you going to follow me inside the bathroom, too?"

"Hey, brother, I mean no disrespect. But you know, there's a *lot*...of people on this plane. So, I just wanna make sure you are going to the restroom, and not the cockpit," I replied.

After seventeen hours and some minutes, our plane finally arrived in Nairobi. I can't remember the name of the airport where we landed. Even if I could, folks, I won't be able to pronounce its name, and I don't know the spelling either. Nevertheless, I was happy we had landed safely. I turned to the guy who looked like Bin Laden and said, "Congratulations, brother. We made it. Welcome to Africa."

The guy replied, "Sir, Africa is a continent. This is Kenya."

I said, "Whatever."

I stepped out of the plane thinking I would be welcomed with that song I mentioned earlier: "*Nantsssssss ingonyama bagithi Baba. Sithi uhm ingonyama. Siyo Nqoba. Ingonyama nengw' enamabala.*" Such was not the case. But in my head, I heard it as I walked to the immigration checkpoint.

Nothing dramatic happened during my check-in, except the lights went off twice without any explanation. And keep in mind that the temperature outside was 99.9 degrees Fahrenheit. No country is perfect; therefore, I'll reserve the 0.1 degree until I get to Jamaica.

When I stepped outside of the airport, I took off my jacket and hailed a cab. I looked at the front and rear of the green cab that came to pick me up, as I had never seen that make and model before. It had a taxi sign on it though, so I hopped inside. The taxi driver was nice, and his service was great until he told me how much it would cost to drop me off at my hotel: five hundred shillings. I said, "Five hundred what? From here to my destination is less than five miles. I checked it on Google Maps before I left America."

"Sir, GPS doesn't work in Nairobi. Besides, do you know how much five hundred shillings is in dollars?" the driver replied.

"No, I don't. How much is it?"

"That's three dollars. Do you have three dollars?"

I was embarrassed and surprised at the same time, 'cause when he mentioned the words "five hundred", I assumed it was a lot of money.

Long story short, I gave him twenty dollars, and told him to keep the change. He was happy, and started driving.

On the first left upon leaving the airport's road, there was a red traffic light. I was expecting him to slow down, but he kept on driving fast.

"Red light, red light, red light!" I blurted out.

He didn't slow down one bit—he just went right through the damn light. I said, "Man, you just ran a red light back there."

"We don't obey traffic lights here," the driver replied.

"Why?"

"None of the lights work," he said.

I didn't know what to say.

Just as he ran another red light, I saw a huge, nice hotel to our left. I exclaimed, "There goes my hotel."

"Not that one. We will soon get to yours. You are going to Guatemala Hotel, right?"

"Yeah, that's the one I booked online," I replied.

We drove another quarter mile, and I saw another beautiful hotel ahead. Again, I asked, "Is that my hotel?"

"No. Not this one, either. Yours is coming up next." I relaxed, and after another mile or so, the driver drove us towards a building that resembled a Motel 6.

"Where're we going bro?" I asked. "This is it—this is Guatemala Hotel," he replied.

"No way. The picture I saw on the internet is different from what's before us. This hotel doesn't look like a five-star hotel." "Yes, it is—for malaria." Now, fellas, I became upset in that moment. As I was getting ready to exit the taxi, I thought "malaria" was another hotel—one smaller than the Guatemala. If I had known, I would have asked him to explain what he was referring. I didn't know it was a common illness in Africa, caused by mosquito bites. I had to find out the hard way just how smart African mosquitos were. Unlike American mosquitos, which introduce themselves by buzzing into your ears before they bite you, African mosquitos make no such introduction. They operate like Navy SEALs. They'll come in quietly, bite you without warning, and exit without detection. And Guatemala Hotel happens to be their headquarters due to the river and waterfall next to it. The lady at the lobby gave me my room key, and told me to always keep my window closed. In America, when you check into a hotel, they'll tell you to always keep your door closed. So, in my mind, I thought that she may have meant the door. I didn't ask. I collected my room key, went to my room, took a shower, and came back downstairs to take a walk outside. As I was walking through the lobby and heading towards the exit, the lady at the front desk said, "Sir, don't play with black mambas."

"I won't," I replied with a laugh. I thought her expression of "don't play with black mambas" was advice to any American who played basketball. To a Lakers fan, "the Black Mamba" is Kobe Bryant's nickname. I didn't know she was talking about one of the most venomous snakes in Africa. If you are paying any close attention to my story thus far, you will have noticed that I had been given three strong warnings about things I didn't understand: malaria, window, and black mamba.

Around 9 p.m., I got back to my hotel room on the seventh floor. From my window, I saw the gorgeous sight of the full moon, beaming over the waterfall. I wanted to cherish and celebrate that moment of my being in the motherland. What other way could one do that, other than to open the window, enjoy the sight of the full moon over the waterfall, while listening to the Lion King's "Circle of Life"? So, that's exactly what I did. I popped the window open for approximately ten minutes while the song played.

I was enjoying the view of the full moon over the waterfall. Meanwhile, unbeknownst to me, all the mosquitos in the area were already inside my bedroom, waiting for my foreign ass to lay down.

Remember, I said earlier that African mosquitos operate like Navy SEALs. Thus, I didn't know I had received several bites while I was asleep. I only discovered them after I woke up the next morning. Every part of my body itched.

I ran to the lobby. As soon as the manager saw me heading towards the front desk—scratching my entire body—she knew exactly what had happened. Before I could say anything, she said, "Sir, it looks like you have been bitten by mosquitos. Did you open your window?" "Yeah, but I closed it after I was done looking at the waterfall. And before I slept, I didn't notice any mosquitos in my room," I replied. With her African accent, she said, "Oh my goodness. Sir, the mosquitos in Africa are smarter than humans. They don't warn before they bite. They bite first and ask questions later. Sir, you have to see a doctor before you develop malaria."

That was when I realized malaria was an illness, not a hotel. She continued: "The person who checked you in yesterday should have told you not to open your window. That's why we have at least two AC units in all our rooms. Who checked you in when you arrived?"

I didn't remember her name, but I remembered that she had said something about black mambas, so I assumed she must have been a Lakers fan.

"She's short, dark-skinned. I think she's a Lakers fan."

"A Lakers fan!" she exclaimed.

She was silent for a moment. Then, she turned around and called out to someone. The lady who had checked me in the night before came out of the back office.

"Hey, good morning." I said.

She looked at me, surprised, and then asked what had happened to me. Before I could say anything else, the manager asked, "Imodu, did you tell this man you are a Lakers fan?"

"No, I didn't tell anyone I was a Lakers fan. I prefer soccer," Imodu replied.

I told the manager, "I'm sorry, ma'am. She didn't tell me she was a Lakers fan. She just joked about the Black Mamba."

Imodu said, "I wasn't joking about black mambas, sir. I was warning you not to play with them."

"*Them*? What do you mean by 'them'?" I asked.

"Sir, you've never heard of the snake called the black mamba?" the manager replied.

"Oh shit. You were referring to a snake?"

"Yes. There are lot of them around here. Black mambas are everywhere," Imodu clarified.

I was scared as shit because I don't like snakes, especially venomous ones.

I said, "Ma'am, black mambas are not everywhere. You said it as if black mambas were omnipotent. I'm from Washington, D.C. The only place you can find a black mamba in D.C. is the zoo."

"Well, sir, welcome to the zoo. Just make sure you don't play with a mamba if you happen to come across one."

Some hours later, I met with a doctor at a local hospital, and he gave me some prescriptions. The doctor happened to have studied in the United States. We had a good time talking to each other. He told me his wife would be celebrating her fiftieth birthday that evening at 5 p.m. He invited me to the party, and gave me the address and his cell phone number.

The hall where the celebration was to take place was inside one of the nice hotels I had seen on my drive from the airport the day before. I promised him I would attend. We shook hands, and I left the hospital.

At 5 p.m. that evening, I was the first to arrive at the hall. The place was empty. In my mind, I thought that I may have had the wrong address. But I couldn't have been wrong. The celebrant's name was printed in bold letters at the entrance of the hall.

Half an hour later, I was still there by myself, waiting for people to arrive. I fell asleep, until at exactly 6:20 p.m., a member of the hotel cleaning crew woke me up and looked at me as though I was crazy.

"What?" I asked.

"Sir, where are you from?"

"I'm from America. Why?"

"What time were you told be here?"

"At 5 p.m. I've been waiting for more than an hour. I don't know what's going on."

"Sir, have you heard of African time?"

"No. What does that mean?"

"It means you are too early. If an African tells you his party starts at 5 p.m., do not arrive until 7 p.m. It's only then that people will start coming in."

I almost started crying like a little baby. I thought to myself, "Hell no. Not again. This is the fifth time within forty-eight hours I've been fooled in Africa."

First, I embarrassed myself over a three-dollar cab fee. Second, I thought malaria was a hotel. Third, I left my window open and got bitten by special forces mosquitos. Fourth, I confused a snake with Kobe Bryant. And now, I was learning about African time too late… *from a cleaner!* Folks, before you go to Africa, ask questions…

Another country I've been to is Jamaica. Peace be unto Bob Marley. Jerk chicken and Bob Marley are the only two things I know about Jamaica.

I don't know why I thought Jamaica was another country that was located far from the United States. Folks, if you stand on the peak of

Panorama Tower in Central Florida, you might possibly see downtown Kingston from there. That's how close Jamaica is to Florida.

I got on the plane, thinking I was going to have a long nap throughout my flight. Unlike my flight to Africa, I wasn't worried about terrorists this time. And the reason was simple. Why? Terrorists don't go to Jamaica. There are only three types of people traveling to Jamaica: Jamaicans, tourists, and drug dealers. Never in the history of the world have I heard of a person who was born and raised in Jamaican that committed suicide. Things like suicide are naturally absent in the Jamaican culture. Thus, if anything happened to our plane, I knew it would be either due to the pilot having fallen asleep, or a bird having flown into an engine.

Less than two hours after we took off from Miami Airport, a violent shake woke me up. My mind is so bad, y'all. I woke up thinking our plane had just landed on water. I must have looked terrified when I asked the Jamaican woman sitting beside me what had just happened. With a Jamaican accent, she replied, "Calm down, man. We just landed in Montego Bay."

"*Bay*? I'm not going to the 'bay'—my destination is Jamaica!"

"Montego Bay is in Jamaica, man. We *are* in Jamaica. Is this your first time here?" she asked.

Before I could reply, everybody on the plane started clapping, as the plane came to a complete stop. I just pretended I knew where the fuck I was, and started clapping too.

We all got off the plane. I don't know how to describe this airport's reception, but something was weird about it. I'm used to the TSA in American airports, and them checking for contraband, like firearms and illegal drugs. These folks in Montego Bay weren't looking for any of that. Instead, "Judy" was busy investigating shit that had nothing to do with immigration—shit like the reason I have two chargers if I only have one phone. She wanted to know why I owned a MacBook, an iPad, an iPhone, and an Apple watch.

And the drama didn't end there. She took out all my colognes and body sprays, and decided she had to test all of them. I asked her why they had to be tested, and she explained to me the experience they had had with people who tried to smuggle heroin in cologne bottles. I didn't have anything illegal, so I took a seat and allowed them to do their job.

I was told the colognes had to be taken to a specialist, who would then test them. For the record, "specialist" in Jamaica doesn't necessarily mean an expert. The "specialist" who was going to test the colognes was an ordinary person who volunteered to have the colon sprayed on his face and neck to perceive the odor. But unfortunately for this person, when Judy grabbed all the colognes from my bag, she mistakenly grabbed my pepper spray as well. You can figure out what happened next.

Five minutes later, I saw five people running down the escalator and in my direction. One of them was holding Judy in his arms, as she gasped for air. As soon as I saw them, I knew something had gone wrong. When they got close to me, one of the men said, "*Ya man…*"

That was all I understood. I did not understand any other word that came out of his mouth.

I was like, "Yo, calm down, man. What happened?"

It was then that he took out my pepper spray. "What kind of perfume is this, man? Me never see one of this perfume before in my life, man."

"Oh shit. Man, that's not a perfume. That's my pepper spray. Is that what happened to Ms. Judy?"

Judy was on the floor, coughing, crying and sneezing at the same time. So, I turned to her and said, "Ms. Judy, I thought you said you were taking my colognes to a specialist for a drug test."

With heavy breaths and a thick Jamaican accent, Judy coughed as she replied, "Me that specialist, man. Me the supervisor, me the security, and me also that specialist, man. Please, don't let me die. Give me the antidote…"

I will quickly talk about some delightful things before I resume telling jokes. At your place of work, school, gym, or where you do your grocery shopping, I'm sure there's at least one vending machine. Vending machines are like saviors when you are thirsty or hungry, and you had not brought any food or drinks from home.

In fact, millions of people around the world depend on vending machines for food daily. But did you know around nineteen percent of vending machine owners make millions of dollars annually? And the reason is because most vending machine owners only depend on the product in their vending machine to make money. In addition, all vending machine owners can increase profit by applying a simple idea: advertisements.

This is not new information. Most vendors just haven't thought about it. But think about it— aren't the three seconds or more that a person spends in front of a vending machine when they are waiting for their food and change the same three seconds one spends watching an ad on YouTube before the video plays? I believe vendors would make more money if they changed the glass of their vending machines to digital touchscreen displays where snacks, drinks, and ads could be seen by customers.

Alright. A word to the wise is enough. Let me get back to jokes.

I mentioned earlier that the fear of my mum is the beginning of wisdom. That was when I was younger. Now that I'm a grown man, I believe the fear of the police is the beginning of wisdom. I thought I was the only one with this fear, until I realized all Americans are directly and indirectly afraid of the police. For instance, when you are driving a car in America and you happen to look in your rear-view mirror and see a police car behind you—whether you are white, black, green, or yellow—there's an unnecessary feeling of guilt in your heart.

I was telling my friend Dave about this the other day, and he kept arguing with me. While we were driving and having this conversation, Dave was speeding. Out of nowhere, a state trooper pulled up behind us, and I was the first to see him.

"Oops! Speak of the devil, Dave—there's a cop behind us."

He looked in the rear-view mirror.

"Fuck."

As soon as he said that, he slowed down. Since he was in the fast lane, I told him to switch to the next lane, so other cars could go past. Dave was reluctant.

"What, are you scared?" I asked him.

"Nope."

"Then move over to the next lane."

"You don't do that, man. The cop will think I'm trying to hide something." Dave reasoned.

"Dave, you are scared. Just admit it."

So, to prove he wasn't scared, Dave switched to the other lane. Guess what happened? The cop followed his ass.

"Damn. Man, I told you! When a cop is behind you, there are two things you don't do. One, you don't speed; and two, you don't change lanes."

"No, Dave. There are two things you are not

doing because a cop is behind you. One, you are not moving fast, and two, you are not having A FUCKING ERECTION. Dave, why the hell are you doing forty-five in the middle of the beltway where the posted speed limit is sixty?"

Moment of truth. People's habits follow them wherever they go. While we might never rid ourselves of some embarrassing habits, we can be honest and be ourselves.

Fiction and what we see on television have a huge impact on our lives. Most people will find out the hard way that they're not the next Beyoncé or Batman. Some things are only meant for entertainment. I say this for people who have raised their ego to the point they've forgotten that all humans were created equal.

Fellas, have you ever tried to talk to a lady and she told you, "You are not my type?" Don't worry, guys. Those are the kind of girls who fall asleep and snore in the movie theater.

The girls who act like your presence is insignificant when you try to talk to them are the kind that talk or fart while asleep.

Take away every rule, policy and constitution that governs a human's behavior, and you'll see no difference between an animal and a human.

As precious as life is, it has no value in the hands of death; thus, if you come across a person who is prideful, remind him or her of the origin of species.

Ladies and gentlemen, a human who lacks humility, or who is a person full of pride, is an easy target for humiliation and destruction. Look at dogs, for instance. They got rid of their wild egos, and today, they live with humans in mansions. We feed them, clothe them, and even give them health insurance, whereas the lion— the king of the jungle— is still out there, sleeping in a den.

You will never see a dog in the zoo. You know why? Because they humbled themselves. Yeah...I know lions are the king of the jungle. But I'd rather be dumb and ignorant, and end up as the leader of the free world, than be smart and intelligent and end up like one former first lady.

If Jesus can come down to this world and live among us, who are we to not humble ourselves? What I'm trying to say is that help is available if some people could only get rid of their egos. Time and again, I've bought food from McDonald's to give out to homeless people, and some had the nerve to tell me they don't eat food from McDonald's. A homeless person! I would then explain to them how I had just eaten there, and that there was nothing wrong with the food. No wonder some people end up homeless. Smart people go to McDonald's and to the dollar store to save money. That's why they have a huge savings account. You will be surprised to know that choosing to eat at McDonald's and going to the dollar store marks the major difference between a rich daddy and a poor daddy. Have you ever met a person who calls every restaurant you mention nasty? Pay close attention to these people, and you will notice they are always broke. Put two and two together, and you will understand how they ended up broke in the first place. They don't cut their coats according to size. They want to sleep in a five-star hotel when they know they can't afford it. They always want to wear the latest shoes, the latest watch, and have the latest technology. And their restaurants are all top notch. All these things are good ONLY IF YOU CAN AFFORD THEM. Why the hell would a starving homeless man turn down the best sandwich from McDonald's? As a matter of fact, he didn't even know what I had in the bag.

I would work at McDonald's whenever I needed some extra change. Most people who call a restaurant nasty likely heard it was so from other people, and they kept that mentality. Some have never even tried the food from those restaurants, while others may have only tried one thing that made their stomach sick, and they concluded that everything served by that entire food chain is bad. That's no different from saying that all Chinese people are bad because one Chinese person did something bad to you.

In America, we are so used to lies and lying;

so much so that if you go to a funeral and ask a child who had just lost his parents how he or she is doing, they will reply, "Good." *While crying.*

Also, has anyone ever realized that dating is perhaps the greatest lie ever? I don't know how the dictionary defines the term "dating", but in America, it means two people going out to an overpriced restaurant to find out about each other's true character within five minutes. So, to do well on a date, both parties will need to put on a show. They will wear their best clothes, leave their attitudes at home, and arrive at the agreed-upon location on time—this is the first lie. The second lie is when the guy opens the car door for the lady, and kisses the back of her hand. She will then pretend as though this is what every normal couple does in a parking lot daily. I can go on and on, but I'm sure you are familiar with the boring process that happens during a date. What's most annoying is when they start asking each other questions you would hear in a job interview, that require them to lie if they want to move to the next level.

"Have you ever used any drugs?"

"No."

"Do you have a bad attitude?"

"No."

"Do you go to church every Sunday?"

"Yes."

"Do you love God?"

"Yes."

"Would you describe yourself as a caring man?" Who in the world will answer "no" to that question during a date?

This process of lying often works well for players. When on a date, players know how to act, what to wear, what to say, what to order, how to use the cutlery. What's more is they also know the location of the women's restroom in the restaurant. Ladies, how would they know such a thing? It is because they've been there several times before—they have brought all their previous victims to the same restaurant.

Ghetto girls understands this gimmick. It's for this reason they don't go on dates. Plus, ghetto girls have a very reasonable low self-esteem. In other words, ghetto girls don't have time for bullshit. The moment your ass starts speaking a language they don't understand, you'll hear something like, "You got some money, bae?"

And God forbid if you ever fall in love with a ghetto girl—don't even think of taking her out on a date. She'll embarrass herself, and embarrass you as well. You'll just notice that the twenty-dollar tip you had left on the table mysteriously disappeared after you returned from the bathroom.

So, what should a real date look like? Ladies, a real date takes time—I'm talking months, sometimes even years. That's how long you need to know a person.

Fellas, you will never discover a woman's true character at Red Lobster, if you spend 200 dollars on pasta and lobster and act like a classy guy who knows how to use the cutlery on every date. And ladies, you will never find Mr. Right by simply asking old-fashioned questions you had dug up from the internet. Mr. Wrong also knows the right answers to those questions.

Initially, dates were occasions for people to learn basic things about the person they had just met. But now, every date turns into an archeological research into human psychology.

Ladies, this is how I think you should handle a date for the first time. There are some good men out there. And by that, I mean good men with good hearts—men who are interested in love, and are willing to spend the rest of their lives with you.

That said, most men—including these good men—have no clue as to what a woman wants. That's why we mess up when we are on a date. Remember, I told you earlier that everything a man does is for a woman. Therefore, ladies, when you are going on a date, take charge by letting the man be a man. When you let him be who he is, he will open up to you. You have the power to do it, and I'm going to teach you how.

The first scenario we will cover is when your date comes to pick you up. Unless you're both in high school, he should have a car. So, you come out of your place and walk to his car.

Normally, the guy should come out of the car and open the door for you; but if he doesn't, don't panic. Most men with good hearts didn't learn how to open the door for people; they only learned how to hold a door for strangers.

When you enter his car, you will notice the interior is extra clean. This was on purpose. It is one of the things men do before they pick up a lady they like.

They make sure their car is clean.

While in his car, my advice to you ladies is not to talk unless he asks you a question. If he does, make sure your answers are short, but truthful. Otherwise, just listen. As per the plan, he will drive you to an overpriced restaurant, or perhaps to one of his favorite places. When you arrive at the parking lot of wherever he takes you, wait in the car and see if he opens the door for you. If he doesn't, just step out and follow him. Despite this, he will open the door of the restaurant for you—trust me.

Now, ladies, this is where you start taking

charge of the date. Unless you are hungry, you don't need to go inside the restaurant. Remember, all you want to know on the first date are basic things about him. Tell him, "Let's go back to the car."

At this point, he will likely be wondering what is going on, and he might ask you why. Tell him there's something you would like to say to him, but you would like to do so in private. Ask him to hold your hand. Look him in the eye, and give him a nice smile the whole time you're walking to the car. This time, however, when both of you get to the front passenger door , common sense will tell him to open the door for you. When he does, give him a hug.

There are two things you want to do when you enter his car. Make sure you hold his hand while talking to him. First, you want to appreciate him. Thank him for picking you up, for the courtesy of opening the door for you and for bringing you to an overpriced restaurant. Obviously, don't call the restaurant overpriced; I'm just being a jerk here. Second, you want to ask basic questions, like where he works, how many siblings he has, his favorite color, his favorite food, the religion he practices, etc. Make sure they are simple questions that you want answers to, so that when a person asks you about the guy you just met, you won't look like a fool. Ladies, unless you want the man to put on a show for you, don't ask him if he's caring or not. If you wish to continue dating him, time will answer that question. After he has answered all your questions and you have answered his, and you wish to see him again, tell him to bring you a rose the next time he picks you up. Tell him you will appreciate it. And round up the conversation with his favorite sport. That will get him talking if he has been quiet. If he doesn't like sports, discuss politics. If he's not into politics, talk about religion. If he doesn't have a religion, talk about science. If he's not into science, doesn't have a religion, indifferent to politics, and doesn't like sports—ladies, I urge you to get out of his car and run, because YOU JUST DATED A SERIAL KILLER.

Ladies and gentlemen, as you know, things aren't what they used to be. Times have changed, and the internet is out of control. Back then, before your video could be played on the internet, you could skip the ad after three seconds. But now they don't give a fuck. Ads have gone wild. Whether you like it or not, you are forced to watch the entire advertisement before you can watch your video. I thought that was crazy, until I discovered how the internet has evolved to the point wherein it can read people's minds.

Have you ever had a question and decided to search the internet for the answer? Let's say you are pondering over the question, "Who is the richest man in the world?" The moment you've typed the third word of that sentence into the search engine, the exact question you had in mind will have likely popped up in the dropdown list of the search bar. If you don't believe me, take a moment to give it a try.

Here is the part where the internet has gotten *really* insane. All of us have had a Facebook page at one point or another; we've all been there. Even Jesus has a Facebook page. This blue part of the internet has become a stage where anyone can go into your cellphone's picture gallery and make your recent picture appear on their site with a private message saying, "Only you can see this picture. Do you want to post this picture on Facebook?" Like, really! Unless I'm mad, why in the world would I want to post a naked picture of myself on the internet? Imagine if your five-year-old was the one who picked up your phone and mistakenly posted the picture. For the geniuses reading this, I understand my given consent to Facebook's app to access or manage my photos and contacts—I don't need a lecture on the US Constitution. However, I know if this becomes an argument, common sense will prevail. My point is that if the internet wants to start a fire, I don't expect the girls in blue to be the people adding fuel to the fire. The internet has enough naked pictures already. Nobody wants to see my naked, ugly, shapeless ass on Facebook.

Let's talk about POLITICS! Oh, you

thought I had forgotten? No, I didn't. I was just waiting for the right time to discuss it.

Some years ago, I was invited to speak to members of Congress. The President and First Lady were also present. Before I started my speech, I said, "I'd like to start by singing the national anthem."

I was flipping through the pages of a book that I had in front of me, as everyone was getting up from their seats. This continued for another five minutes after everybody had stood up. As they were waiting and wondering what was keeping me, an agent approached me hurriedly and whispered in my ear, "Sir, what's going on? Are you going to sing the national anthem, or what?"

"I can't sing the national anthem. I don't even know the words." I replied.

The agent was stunned. Keep in mind that everybody in the room was listening in to our conversation, as I had planted a secret microphone on my shoulder hours earlier.

The agent replied, "Sir, if you knew you

couldn't sing the national anthem, why then did you make the President and members of Congress stand up for over five minutes?"

I turned to the audience, and spoke directly into the microphone on the podium.

"I just wanted them to know how we feel when they promise to do something for us, and they fail to keep their promise. Just like everybody in this room who's waiting for me to sing the national anthem, I'm also still waiting for the universal healthcare they had promised us a decade ago. Ladies and gentlemen, if you can, please have a seat."

Politicians are like players. I should have dedicated the title of this book to them.

Where in the world is the Obama family? Do First Families disappear after the president's term is over? You've got to love them. President Obama must be the only US president who knows more about the history of every other country than its own citizens. The guy is so cool. At one point in 2009, the presidential campaign got so real that Obama didn't know who he was campaigning against: a plumber or a war hero.

When he became the President, the Secret Service were concerned, especially regarding his first trip to Afghanistan to visit our troops. When it came time for him to address the Afghan press, the Secret Service told him the only thing he had to worry about was a shoe thrower.

"I'm not going to worry about that. I can catch a pass," replied Obama.

The year 2016 came along, and it was time for another presidential campaign. I was ready for it, and so were the kids—we were all seated in the living room, waiting for it to start. However, we didn't know that CNN had a surprise for us all; the campaign's broadcast was rated PG-13. Unaware of the change in rating, I turned on the TV, and the first thing I heard was, *"Grab 'em by the pussy."* When my girl heard the "P" word, she ran from the kitchen to the living room. By then, I had already turned off the television.

"Baby, why are you watching Jerry Springer in

front of the kids?" she asked.

"Baby, I need you to take the kids upstairs," I replied.

The kids started crying.

"Why can't we stay and watch the campaign with you?" they kept asking. "It's just a campaign, right?"

"Well, that's what I thought, boys. But it looks like this year's campaign is about to get real," I explained.

After my girl and the kids went upstairs, I turned the TV back on, and all I heard was, "*Security....get 'em out of here. Throw 'em out. Lock 'em up. I'll pay the legal fee. Out, out, out, out, out, out, out.*"

My girlfriend, on her way back to the kitchen, yelled at me.

"WHY ARE YOU WATCHING JERRY SPRINGER WHEN THE PRESIDENTIAL CAMPAIGN IS ON?"

I shouted back. "BABY, YOU NEED TO COME HERE QUICKLY, AND SEE WHAT I'M LOOKING AT. THIS YEAR'S CAMPAIGN HAS GONE WILD."

I thought black people gave the strangest handshakes—until Trump came along. For those of you who don't know, before any new handshake is introduced to the world, black people must first test it to make sure it's safe for distribution. Folks, the handshake you see Trump giving to world leaders on television has not yet been tested by black people. The Japanese Prime Minister was the first to get a taste of that unregistered handshake. When he reached out for it, every black person watching at home was saying, "Shinzo, don't do it, don't do it, don't do it!" But he didn't listen. He almost lost his arm on national television. The following day, the press asked Mr. Trump why he almost gave the Japanese Prime Minister a stroke, and he replied with his standard answer: "Fake news..."

But did you know Trump was the first candidate in the history of the world who didn't lie during his political campaign? Think about it. He's the first candidate in the history of politics who talks first and thinks later. If you ask another politician a question, often, they'll start their answer with, "I think"—an expression Trump is not used to. Furthermore, a clever politician whose plans is to build a wall and to get Mexico to pay for it will wait until after Mexico has finished paying for it before revealing the plan. That's how Obama was able to catch Bin Laden. He didn't tell anyone until the operation was over. That's how Congress was able to make China pay for the war in the Middle East. Oh, you think George Bush didn't understand what he was saying when he said, "The Iraq war will pay for itself." A smart cobra doesn't fight its prey. That's the job of its venom.

After George Bush had used the Chinese's money to liberate Iraq, can you guess who is benefiting most from Iraqi oil? China. You don't tell Mexico ahead of time that you intend to build a wall and make them pay for it. That's not how politics works. That's like sticking your bare hand in a viper's hole to find out if the snake is at home. Everyone knows there's only one thing Mexicans don't like to build: walls. And the reason is because, for some genetic reason, the

Mexicans' growth hormones make them naturally afraid of heights. You can call Mexicans for road, house, and sidewalk construction, and *all of them* will show up at 2:45 a.m. Just don't call them for wall construction; that's the only thing Mexicans won't help you build.

Let me touch on other "fake news" before I end our discussion on politics. How many people has Trump fired so far—365? He fired the FBI director one day, and called the FBI headquarters the next to ask to speak to the FBI director.

Whoever answered the phone said, "You fired him yesterday, sir. We are still waiting for you to send us a new director. When should we expect him or her?"

"As soon as Jackie Chan gets back to me. He's who I chose to be the new FBI director. He knows how to fight the bad guys," the President replied.

The President always gives a speech after a bad incident happens. How that works is the Press Secretary will gather the names of all the victims involved, and hand over the list to the President. The President will then write his speech around those names. So, Mr. President selected three names of the four officers who died at the Texas border, and wrote his own speech. God bless our border patrol officers.

At the State of the Union, the President began his speech. "There's no other agency in America that bears more risk than our beautiful border patrol agents." The audience gave a round of applause. "They work tirelessly, day and night, to make sure our communities are safe from drugs, gangs, and illegal immigrants pouring into our beautiful country through our border. While these agents do their best to keep us safe, sometimes they lose their lives in the process. Today, we are going to honor Officer Gary Castro, Officer Paul Mandy, and Officer Jeff Nicolas. Three great men and brave Americans, who gave their lives at the front line defending the country they love. On June 3, 2020, a white truck carrying four passengers was stopped at the US border in Hale County, Texas, based on a tip received by authorities. The four men in the vehicle were ordered to exit the car by a border patrol officer. As the four men got out of the car, three of them opened fire, before they took off running. Officer Gary, Paul, and Jeff immediately ran after them, but along the way, the four bad guys opened fire again, and these three young officers were killed. These men are great Americans who wanted to make America great again. They gave their service, and gave their lives to defend us. Please, I need a Secret Service agent to pull up their pictures on the big screen behind me, as we all stand up to honor them."

For the record, this was the first time the President saw the pictures of the officers to whom he was referring.

As every member of Congress in the room stood up, the pictures of three K9 German shepherds wearing badges appeared on the projector screen behind the President. Under each picture was a name: Gary, Paul, and Jeff. To the President and everyone's surprise, the three officers to whom the President had been referring as "men" were not human. Gary, Paul, and Jeff were K9 officers who died alongside of their fellow human officers. Ladies and gentlemen, it's a great thing to become a leader, but there's nothing great about a leader who doesn't understand what the hell he or she is talking about.

You've got to be careful to whom you listen these days, and you especially need to think twice before you do anything anyone asks of you.

One Sunday, my mum and I attended a church in Texas for the first time. It was a beautiful church, with a wonderful choir and great audience. I was sitting, with my mum beside me, and everyone was ready, anxiously waiting for the pastor to preach. Finally, the pastor arrived, and everyone in the church stood up. The pastor stepped on the pulpit, lifted his Bible, and said, "Raise your Bible up, and say after me." So, all of us in attendance raised up their Bibles. The pastor continued.

"Say it like you mean it: 'This is my Bible.

I'm what it says I am. I have what it says I have. I can do what it says I can do. Today, I'll be taught the word of God. I boldly confess. My mind is alert. My heart is receptive. I'll never be the same, in Jesus' name'."

Everyone in the church recited those words after the pastor, except me. My mum noticed I stayed quiet while the pastor spoke, and she waited until we were seated before talking to me. As soon as we sat, she leaned over.

"Why didn't you say what the pastor asked everyone to say?" she asked as she whispered into my left ear.

I leaned towards her and whispered back.

"First, Mum, this Bible in my hand ain't mine. I stole it from my roommate. Second, I haven't read the entire Bible; so, I don't know 'everything it says I am'. Some things might be good, and some might not be—I don't know. I like to read and understand before I consent to anything. And third, Mum, you know damn well we ain't got what the Bible says we have. We are broke as hell. Lastly—"

Before I could give her my last reason, she stopped me.

"Enough. Why do you always have to say something smart when people are serious? I don't know where in my womb you got your mouth from. You just messed up my Sunday," she said.

"Mum, I'm not finished—" I replied.

"Enough! Boy, if I hear one more word from your mouth, I'll whip your ass in front of everybody in this church." And when my mum says she's going to whip your ass—trust me, she's going to do it. It doesn't matter where you are. So, I kept quiet.

I'll never forget the day I traveled with my mum on the plane for the first time. I don't remember what I had done wrong that made her whip my ass so bad. When the lady beside us couldn't take it anymore, she called 911 at 30,000 feet above the ocean. My mum waited for the lady to finish the phone call and whipped her ass too.

Can someone tell me how the heck they found

Bin Laden, but they still can't find X? Or have any of you found X yet? If the FBI and the CIA still can't find X, how do our math teachers think we were going to find it in a classroom? They've been looking for it since my father was in kindergarten, and my math teacher had the nerve to come to my class the other day at college and ask me to find X.

Back then, when I was in class, the moment I would hear the word "find," my mind would go somewhere else. I would lean over, and start looking under and around my seat. I would stand up, and check all my pockets. Once, as I was about to empty my backpack, my math professor asked, "Mr. Teni, what are you looking for?"

"X," I replied.

He said, "It's right here on the board."

Angrily, I replied, "If the shit is right there on the board, sir, then why the heck did you ask me to find it?" He threw me out of the class immediately. The next day, I brought a bag of alphabet cookies with me to class in case he asked us to find another letter.

Quickly, I'm going to drop a tip for every parent before I continue telling jokes. Back in the day, when I was growing up, there were no cellphones, laptops, or tablets. There were land phones and pagers; but from where I came, only rich people used them. One or two libraries in the area had a desktop computer, if you wanted to use one and were willing to walk a mile. So, in those days, most kids depended on books, teachers, and their parents to answer their questions. Today, things have changed. With the help of technology, anyone with a cellphone can access the world in the palm of their hand. An easy method of learning that most parents haven't yet realized. Parents, if your child can read and has access to the internet via the phone you bought for them, the next time you ask them a question, don't take no for an answer. If your child knows how to use Facebook and Twitter, they should know how to search for answers on the web. If your child can't type, they can speak and use Google Voice Search. Show them. If you show your child how to conduct their own research at an early age, it will help them later in life. Suddenly, your fifth grader who wants to become a doctor in the future will realize they don't have to wait until tenth grade before they can start learning the basics of biology. The internet is full of knowledge, and it is available to anyone who is willing to search. Let's get back to jokes.

There are some questions that baffle me. Maybe some of you have also wondered about them. They consist of the following:

Why are the things we don't need always easy to find, but when we finally need them, they're suddenly like a needle in a haystack?

Why do fat people drive trucks?

Why do people like to come close at the exact moment you fart?

Why do we constantly see our deceased loved ones in our dreams?

If God didn't intend for humans to have sex in the beginning, what then was the purpose of Adam's penis and Eve's vagina?

Why do hockey players fight?

Why is the hood always dark at night, even when the lights are on?

Why do eighty percent of Hispanic males work in construction?

What mother named her son Tiger?

Why do they serve us fortune cookie trays at the buffet when we're not ready to leave?

If vegetables are healthy, why aren't cows skinny?

What do vegans prepare for Thanksgiving?

What benefit do people get from smoking?

Is gravity a force or a curvature in space?

Who do gay people pray to?

Do aliens exist?

How did Trump become president?

Who lives in Antarctica?

How does a plane fly?

And why is it that everything a human likes from the depths of their heart, is said to be bad for them? Take the following examples and their apparent effect on us:

Sodas? They contain too many calories.

Steak? They cause high blood pressure.

Guns? They are dangerous.

Fried food? It's unhealthy.

Burgers? They can cause heart attacks.

Liquor? It's bad for your liver.

Cigarettes? They're bad for your lungs.

Weed? It's bad, but we don't know why.

Crack? It can make you go crazy.

Fornication? It's a sin.

Playing video games all day? You are not serious.

Driving fast? It's dangerous.

Sleeping until 10 a.m.? You are broke.

But guess what? Everything we hate from the depths of our heart is said to be good for us. Shit like running, stopping at the stop sign at two o'clock in the morning, eating vegetables, reading books, drinking a lot of water, driving slow, not eating after 8 p.m., waking up as early as 4 a.m., taking a shower with cold water, not cursing even if you are upset, not playing loud music, not lying, not drinking alcohol, not smoking, not gambling, turning your right cheek to someone after they've slapped your left cheek. Like, really? And they wonder why some people are retarded. Why wouldn't they be? Show me a person who obeys all these so-called "good things" listed above, and I will show you a retard.

I asked earlier why fat people drive trucks. It's just something I had noticed. Why? I don't know. But you've got to love fat people. I love 'em. And that's because I used to be one of them. We know where all the buffets in town are located. If you are new in town, and you don't know how to get to the nearest buffet, just look for a fat person. They'll give you directions.

Fat people do some funny stuff, though. They will go to the gym with a gallon of Gatorade, walk for twenty minutes on the treadmill, and then attempt to lift weights they obviously can't lift. On their way home, they'll stop at 7-Eleven and buy a large Slurpee. When they get home, they'll take a shower, dress nice, and head to the buffet. After they've eaten all the wings and fries, they'll ask for a Diet Pepsi. Why? They are watching their weight.

There's one more thing I'd like to touch on before I continue. Fat people, if you go to

McDonald's and you order a salad with bread crumbs, sliced egg, bacon, shredded cheese, grilled chicken, onions, tomatoes, and ranch salad dressing—you might as well order a large fries and vanilla shake, because you just ordered the ingredients of a burger.

The funniest day of my life was the day I ran into my personal trainer at the buffet. He said, "Mr. Teni, what are you doing here?"

"Same thing you are," I replied.

He said, "I'm just here to pick up a couple of salads."

"Me too," I quickly fired back.

He stared at the heavily loaded plate I was about to devour and said, "That food in your hand doesn't look like salad." "You haven't heard about wing salad, General Tso's salad, barbecue pork salad, fried rice salad, or steak and cheese salad? Bro, as long as there's vegetable in a food—it's all salad to me."

Ladies, if you are not a celebrity—in other words,

you are not a famous singer, you are not the first lady of any country, you don't play any sport whatsoever, and you are not married to a prince from England—and more than five thousand people are following you on various social media, you've got a huge problem. And this "problem" is the reason these strangers follow you—it is either in front of you or behind you. I know this because my girlfriend is also suffering from one of these huge problems, too. Not only has she exceeded the total numbers of followers allowed on Facebook she also has four personal trainers; all of whom volunteered to train her for free. Guys, isn't that amazing? Don't ask me why—I don't know. Maybe it's because she has a fat ass—I don't know.

Then, I decided I was going to find out. So, one day, I followed her to the gym. I told her not to introduce me to anyone when we got there, and to just go ahead and work out, and to let me work out alone. She agreed. I was in the gym working out, while my girl and this dude named James were on the other side of the room doing their workout session.

From the treadmill on which I was running, I could hear the personal trainer calling all kinds of workout moves to my girlfriend. I didn't understand any of them. There was one called "abs dug." He made my girl lie on her back. Then he held her legs up and moved them like scissors. I watched them at the corner of my eye, but acted like I wasn't concerned.

They kept on going, shifting from one move to another. It was almost like watching my girl doing porn with another man. Finally, he called out a move that forced me to go over to where they were, and introduce myself. This move was called "butt firm." Fellas, I've never heard *butt firm* before, I don't know if it's a real workout, or if a pervert made it up. My girl knelt in the doggy position, and the trainer was behind her. With one hand, he would help her lift her legs one after the other, while the other held down her waist.

As soon as this provocative workout started, I tapped the dude on the back, and introduced myself to him. He was nice to me, telling me how my girl had been improving her weight loss. I asked if he was married, and he said he was.

"Oh, good. Why don't you bring your wife tomorrow, so we can all work out together?" I replied.

He agreed. Some minutes later, we shook hands and left the gym.

The next day at around 4 p.m., we all met again at the gym. His wife looked good—she was a tall, light-skinned lady. My plan was simple. I knew he was going to train my girlfriend as usual. In return, I requested to train his wife too. I told him about it, and he agreed.

The workout began. I had no clue how to train another person, but I was listening to him as he called out moves to my baby. So, everything he did to my girl, I did the same to his.

Finally, he called out the name of a workout that would raise any man's suspicion. I quickly searched for the workout on the internet, but Google didn't return any results. So, I decided to get smart too. I turned to his wife and said,

"Ma'am, the next workout we are going to do is called *'grab 'em by the pussy.'* Let me show you how it's done."

The personal trainer looked in my direction and said, "Grab em by the *what?*"

I turned to face him.

"Oh, you won't understand that workout, bro. It's the latest workout in the White House. It's an exclusive presidential workout. Only two people in the world know how to administer it: me and the Commander in Chief."

"No...man. Stop playing with me, bro. There's no such workout with the name 'grab them by the pussy'."

"Neither is *butt firm*," I replied with humor. "This is my seventh time searching for it on the internet, and Google still can't find a result for it."

If you think you are smart—well, two can play at that game.

Why do Christians always lie at people's funerals? One evening, during a funeral in Chicago, a reverend said something so funny, that the dead body in the coffin rose and laughed.

"A life well lived. Another great soldier has gone home. I know Brother Moses is in heaven resting in the blessed hand of the Lord."

For the record, "Brother Moses" was killed by the police during a firefight, after he had robbed a bank and shot an old lady in the leg. Now, fellas, I don't know if hellfire has another cool name, but the last time I checked, bank robbers don't go to heaven.

Imagine walking into heaven and the first person you bump into is Hitler! You're likely to walk right back to the heavenly gate, and ask the angels some questions.

"Excuse me, Gabe—I don't mean no disrespect, but y'all don't take bribes over here, right?"

"No. What's wrong?" Angel Gabriel would likely reply.

"Is this heaven or hell?"

"This is heaven. Is there a problem, sir?"

"Yeah, there is a big problem—and it's right here in heaven. Gabriel, I need to talk to Jesus

ASAP. Heaven can't be this rough. That's not what I had read in the Bible."

If a public restroom door is locked, there are only two reasons why that would be. One, there's someone inside the restroom; or two, the key to the restroom door is with the cashier. It is so annoying when you're using the restroom and someone starts knocking on the door. After they've knocked and jiggled the handle several times, they'll then ask a stupid question.

"Is someone in there?"

Dude, if the door is locked, it means there's someone in there. Right? If not, go to the cashier and ask them for the key!

Then they'll reply, "I'm sorry."

I hate that statement. There are two statements I hate to hear—"I'm sorry" and "Thank you." Anytime I hear either of those statements, either someone just messed up or something big just came out of my wallet.

When I was preparing to write this book, my plan was to write jokes that were out of this planet—something different, I thought. But I encountered a problem. How could I write jokes about a planet I hadn't been to before? I thought about the moon. What could I say about the moon that would make people laugh? Er…did we fake the moon landing? No. Obama already claimed that joke. Then, I gave it a second thought. Did we *actually* fake the moon landing? I had been pondering over this question when I fell asleep on the couch in my living room, with a Playboy magazine on my chest.

As usual, mother nature kicked in. I had a dream. Dave, a Hispanic astronaut and I had just crash-landed on Mars. I was the first to exit our space shuttle, and they followed. What we saw when we got outside was unbelievable. Millions of beautiful women with gold skin stood in a circle about fifty feet away from our damaged shuttle. They stared at us in surprise.

None of them were less than seven feet tall. The ugliest among them was ten times more beautiful than the most beautiful women on earth. And all of them were naked.

Their breasts were triangular and firm,

pointing out of their chests like two vertical pyramids. Their nipples were crystal diamonds, and so were their eyes.

I turned my face to look at Dave and the other astronaut. Both had removed their head protection. Dave's saliva dripped out gently out of the corner of his mouth. Suddenly, Dave slowly moved forward.

"I'm going to say hi to them," he said.

I smacked the son of a bitch on the back of his head and dragged his ass back to where he belonged: the floor.

"Hey, man, why did you do that?!"

"Idiot! You're not gonna embarrass me here, fool. I'm calling the shots today."

The other astronaut interrupted.

"Should we offer them some money?" he asked.

Dave and I looked at his dumb ass, as if to say, "Does this place look like Texas to you, bro? Do you see any Taco Bell around here?"

Out of nowhere, a reddish horse carrying one of the ladies came running behind us. While the three of us turned back to look, the rest of the ladies around our shuttle bowed down. The horse came to a stop not too far from us, and the queen riding it came down. She walked majestically towards me.

Because I was in the middle, that made me look like the leader. She got closer to me, and started sniffing my neck. Folks, I don't know how it happened—but somehow, both my hands just landed on her boobs. I grabbed those alien boobs like the wheel of an eighteen-wheeler. The queen gave me an everlasting slap that immediately sent me back to earth. When I woke up, I felt that both my hands were on a women's chest. I opened my eyes, and saw that the breasts I had grabbed were my mum's, as she had just bent over to wake me up. My mum also gave me an eternal slap that immediately sent me back to the dream. As soon as the queen saw me coming back, she gave me an uppercut. This time, I didn't wake up in the living room—I woke up on the moon in a used Bugatti.

In case you are trying to paint a picture in

your mind of what Dave looks like, let me assist you. You know the people at the gym who run at crazy high speeds on the treadmill? That's Dave. Have you seen a person at the soda machine mixing different kinds of soda in one cup? That's Dave. You know the people that have a good paying job, yet they'll pick up every penny they see on the floor? That's Dave. Ladies, has a guy ever come to you and asked for your number before introducing himself? That's Dave. By now, whether you are a male or female, I believe you should have painted a picture of a complete asshole in your mind. If you have: yep, that's Dave. But he's cool. Except for some caveman logic he often practices that defiles common sense. For instance, Dave is one of many Americans who, because of a 3-cent in price difference, will drive 5 miles to another county to buy gas. He's a childhood friend, though. Those ones are very hard to get rid of, if you know what I mean.

It's also possible that you have been wondering what I look like. I'm the child a former president mentioned several times during his campaign. That skinny kid with a funny name who believes America also has a place for him. Yep! That's me.

If you've read this book all the way from the beginning to this point and you haven't laughed yet, it could be for three reasons. One, you are facing serious criminal charges, and the public defender appointed for you happened to be your ex. Two, you just found out that your spouse and your best friend are dating, and that's the reason why you picked up this book, to console yourself. Three, both reasons above apply to you. If you belong to any of these three categories, the solution to your problem is unfortunately more than a comedian can provide. You don't need a comedian—you need a therapist.

However, whatever the case, remember this: on the day you were born, you cried. But the day you die, people will cry for you. Therefore, while you still have breath in you, why don't you take a moment to laugh and appreciate the little time you have left on Earth? Because it doesn't matter if you accomplish something in this life; every human who came to this world will be certified twice. My first certificate was given to my parents when I was born, and the second will be given to my kids when I'm gone.

I appreciate all of you for taking a moment of your precious time to read this book. The love I have for you is more than the love a monkey has for a banana. I love you like Barack loves Michelle. That doesn't mean I'll catch a grenade for you, though—I don't catch stuff like that.

At the time I wrote this page, the NBA playoffs were on. I'm not interested in watching commercial breaks, so I usually switch to other entertainment when the ads come on. I watched a video on YouTube that made me laugh. I thought to share it with you.

This video is a short documentary about a guy who is looking for love overseas, that I had played at random after I watched a movie trailer. The title of the video is: "Guy spends thousands of dollars trying to find a wife way out of his league overseas." The part that makes me laugh the most is towards the end of the video at the thirteenth-minute mark, so you will have to watch the video from the beginning to get there.

I'll leave you with that video, so that after you close this book, you will continue laughing.

Thank you very much.

"The work of your hand doesn't have to be perfect; it just has to look like it."

—*Teni A.*

www.ingramcontent.com/pod-product-compliance
Lightning Source LLC
Chambersburg PA
CBHW032111040426
42337CB00040B/187